YA ESCRIBIMOS

A Writing Workbook for First-Level Spanish Students

Alice Mohrman Kosnik

National Textbook Company
a division of NTC/CONTEMPORARY PUBLISHING GROUP
Lincolnwood, Illinois USA

ISBN: 0-8442-7019-5

Published by National Textbook Company,
a division of NTC/Contemporary Publishing Company,
4255 West Touhy Avenue,
Lincolnwood (Chicago), Illinois 60646-1975 U.S.A.

8 9 0 ML 9 8 7 6

FOREWORD

Ya escribimos is the ideal workbook for students of Spanish, and may be used from the middle school through college. The book covers the main grammar concepts that are introduced to first-year students and that are commonly reviewed in second-year studies.

Students will get plenty of practice with verbs, since *Ya escribimos* offers a variety of exercises with the past tenses, in addition to the progressive, future, conditional, and compound tenses. Examples and exercises to drill the imperative, expressions of time with *hacer*, and the uses of *hay* and *había* are also included. There are also lessons that review direct and indirect object pronouns, prepositional pronouns, comparison of adjectives, and shortened adjectives. The final lesson deals with Spanish word families, and will increase students' vocabulary through its assortment of suffixes, prefixes, and cognates.

Although the exercises have been arranged in order of difficulty, they also can be used in any sequence in order to accommodate a basal text. The vocabulary is controlled and easily accessible to first- and second-year students. And the interesting exercises and activities—which include word mazes and crossword puzzles—are guaranteed to reinforce grammar that has been presented, or to review structures previously studied. Students will have the chance to write many complete answers to questions and also provide personal responses. *Ya escribimos* really allows students to polish their writing skills!

CONTENIDO

Lección I — EL PRETÉRITO

GRAMÁTICA: Preterite tense of regular -ar, -er, and -ir verbs

I.   The preterite tense is used to indicate a finished action, one that occurred in the past. To form the preterite tense of any regular -ar verb, drop the -ar and add the preterite tense endings. Each ending tells who did the action. Be certain to indicate the accent marks when necessary.

Person	Ending	Example: hablar — to speak	
Yo	-é	hablé	— I spoke, did speak
Tú	-aste	hablaste	— You spoke, did speak
Él, Ella, Ud.	-ó	habló	— He, she, you spoke, did speak
Nosotros	-amos	hablamos	— We spoke, did speak
Ellos, Ellas, Uds.	-aron	hablaron	— They, you spoke, did speak

A.   Write in the blanks the correct preterite tense form of the verb given at the top of each list.

MODELO: *hablar*   Yo _hablé_

1.   *estudiar* — to study

Yo _____

Pedro _____

Uds. _____

Tú y yo _____

Tú _____

2.   *trabajar* — to work

Tú _____

Nosotros _____

Yo _____

Ellos _____

Ud. _____

3.   *comprar* — to buy

Miguel _____

Uds. _____

Tú _____

Yo _____

María y yo _____

4.   *viajar* — to travel

Yo _____

Nosotras _____

Tú _____

Anita _____

Uds. _____

5.   *visitar* — to visit

Ud. _____

Yo _____

Ellas _____

Uds. y yo _____

Tú _____

1

B. Complete the following sentences with the correct form of the verb in parentheses.

MODELO: (hablar) El profesor _habló_ mucho.

1. (trabajar) Ud. _____ mucho.
2. (hablar) Yo _____ español en la clase.
3. (estudiar) Anita y yo _____ para el examen.
4. (cantar) Los alumnos _____ en el coro.
5. (viajar) Tú _____ a México, ¿verdad?
6. (visitar) Mi mamá _____ a su hermana.
7. (desear) Tú y yo _____ ir a California.
8. (llevar) Yo _____ los pantalones nuevos.
9. (comprar) Mis amigos _____ los discos nuevos.
10. (mirar) ¿ _____ tú la televisión anoche?

C. Select the correct subject from the list and write it in the blank.

Yo, Tú, Paco, Susana y yo, Las chicas

MODELO: _Susana y yo_ miramos la televisión anoche.

1. _____ miraron la televisión ayer.
2. _____ viajé a Nueva York.
3. _____ trabajó mucho.
4. _____ deseamos ir al parque.
5. _____ compraron una radio.
6. _____ estudiaste la lección.
7. _____ llevamos pantalones rojos.
8. _____ hablé con el profesor.
9. _____ visitó a Carmen.
10. _____ cantaste muy bien.

D. Rewrite the following sentence. Change the two verbs to agree with each new subject.

MODELO: Paco *viajó* a México y *visitó* las pirámides.
(Mis amigos) _Viajaron a México y visitaron las pirámides._

1. (Yo) _____
2. (Mis padres) _____
3. (Ud.) _____
4. (Tú) _____
5. (Alberto y yo) _____

2

E. Answer the following questions with responses true for you.

MODELO: ¿Hablaste español ayer? <u>Sí, hablé español ayer</u>.

1. ¿Viajaste a México el año pasado?

_____

2. ¿Miró su papá la televisión anoche?

_____

3. ¿Hablaron sus amigos en la clase ayer?

_____

4. ¿Estudiaron Uds. mucho la semana pasada?

_____

5. ¿Visitaste a tus abuelos el mes pasado?

_____

F. Hidden in the maze are all the preterite forms of the following verbs. See if you can find all fifty of them! Words go in all directions.

trabajar   hablar   estudiar   cantar   viajar   visitar
desear   llevar   comprar   mirar

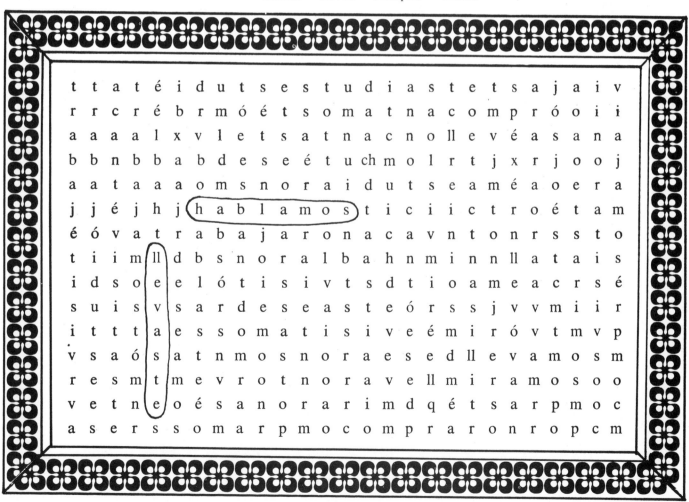

II. To form the preterite tense of any regular *-er* or *-ir* verb, drop the *-er* or *-ir* and add the following endings.

Person	Ending	Example: *vivir* — to live	
Yo	-í	viví	— I lived, did live
Tú	-iste	viviste	— You lived, did live
Él, Ella, Ud.	-ió	vivió	— He, she, you lived, did live
Nosotros	-imos	vivimos	— We lived, did live
Ellos, Ellas, Uds.	-ieron	vivieron	— They, you lived, did live

A. Write in the blanks the correct preterite tense form of the verb given at the top of each list.

MODELO: *beber*   Yo __bebí__

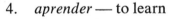

1. *comer* — to eat

   Yo _____

   Tú _____

   Paco _____

   Tú y yo _____

   Uds. _____

2. *correr* — to run

   Los alumnos _____

   Tú _____

   Ana _____

   Yo _____

   Tú y yo _____

3. *escribir* — to write

   Mis amigos _____

   El profesor _____

   Yo _____

   Tú _____

   Nosotras _____

4. *aprender* — to learn

   Ud. y yo _____

   Uds. _____

   Yo _____

   Miguel _____

   Tú _____

5. *salir* — to leave

   Mi papá _____

   Tú _____

   Juan y yo _____

   Yo _____

   Ellos _____

B. Match the subject in list A with a correct phrase from list B. Copy the sentence on the lines below.

List A

1. Uds.
2. Yo
3. Bárbara
4. Tú
5. Miguel
6. Juan y yo

List B

A. comí muchos tacos
B. corriste en la clase de gimnasia
C. escribió una carta
D. vivieron en California
E. aprendió el francés
F. salimos a las 8.00

MODELO: <u>Bárbara aprendió el francés.</u>

1. _____
2. _____
3. _____
4. _____
5. _____

C. In the blanks below write any subject pronoun or name that correctly goes with the verb form.

MODELO: <u>Pedro</u> comió el desayuno.

1. _____ salí a las 9.00.
2. _____ comieron los sándwiches.
3. _____ escribió la lección de historia.
4. _____ aprendiste el francés.
5. _____ comí el almuerzo.
6. _____ corrimos al parque.
7. _____ corrió a la plaza.
8. _____ escribimos una tarjeta postal.
9. _____ salió de la casa.
10. _____ aprendieron a esquiar.

D. Answer the following questions with responses true for you.

MODELO: ¿Aprendiste el francés? <u>No, no aprendí el francés.</u>

1. ¿Comiste mucho ayer? _____

2. ¿Escribieron Uds. las lecciones anoche? _____

3. ¿Vivió su familia en Texas el año pasado? _____

4. ¿Salieron sus padres de la casa a las 8.00? _____

5. ¿Aprendiste a esquiar el año pasado? _____

E. *Crucigrama:* Work the crossword puzzle as you would in English. Use the preterite tense.

HORIZONTALES

1. (comer) Yo _____ un taco.
2. (salir) Tú y yo _____ a las 8.00.
4. (comer) Tú _____ mucho.
9. (comer) Uds. _____ mucho.
11. (escribir) Yo _____ una carta.
13. (aprender) Nosotros _____ mucho.
15. (salir) Uds. _____ a las 9.00.
16. (comer) Nosotros _____ rápidamente.
18. (correr) Yo _____ a la escuela.
20. (salir) Él _____ a las 6.00.
21. (correr) Uds. _____ rápidamente.
22. (aprender) Yo _____ la lección.
23. (comer) Mi hermano _____ mucho.

VERTICALES

1. (comer) Nosotros _____ mucho.
3. (aprender) Ellos _____ mucho.
5. (escribir) Ud. _____ la lección.
6. (salir) Tú _____ a las 10.00.
7. (salir) Yo _____ temprano.
8. (escribir) Nosotros _____ .
10. (aprender) Tú _____ la historia.
12. (escribir) Tú no _____ .
13. (aprender) Paco no _____ nada.
14. (escribir) Ellos _____ en inglés.
17. (correr) Yo _____ a clase.
19. (correr) María _____ al parque.

Lección II — PRETÉRITOS IRREGULARES

GRAMÁTICA: Preterite tense of common irregular verbs

I. Some Spanish verbs are irregular in the preterite tense. The forms of these verbs must be learned separately. The preterite forms of *ir* and *ser* are identical.

Person	Examples:	ir — to go	ser — to be
Yo	fui	I went, did go	I was
Tú	fuiste	You went, did go	You were
Él, Ella, Ud.	fue	He, she, you went, did go	He, she was, you were
Nosotros	fuimos	We went, did go	We were
Ellos, Ellas, Uds.	fueron	They, you went, did go	They, you were

A. Write in the blanks the correct preterite tense form of *ir* or *ser*.

MODELO: (ser) Yo __fui__ el héroe.

1. (ir) Mis amigos _____ a California.
2. (ser) Cristóbal Colón _____ el descubridor de América.
3. (ir) Yo _____ a la tienda anoche.
4. (ser) Tú _____ el héroe del partido.
5. (ir) Mi hermano y yo _____ a la casa de Pedro.
6. (ser) Yo _____ el jefe del grupo.
7. (ir) Paco _____ al parque.
8. (ser) Mis clases favoritas _____ español y gimnasia.
9. (ir) Tú _____ al mercado ayer, ¿verdad?
10. (ser) Mi amigo y yo _____ los líderes del club.

B. Rewrite the following sentence. Change the verb to agree with each new subject.

MODELO: Juan fue a España el verano pasado.

(Mis amigos) _fueron a España el verano pasado._

1. Mi familia _____
2. Yo _____
3. Los señores Méndez _____
4. Tú _____
5. Mis amigos y yo _____

C. Answer the following questions with responses true for you.

MODELO: ¿Adónde fuiste el verano pasado? _Fui a Wisconsin_ .

1. ¿Adónde fuiste el verano pasado?

_____

2. ¿Cuál fue su clase favorita el año pasado?

_____

3. ¿Fueron Uds. a la escuela ayer?

_____

4. ¿Fueron difíciles los exámenes de español?

_____

5. ¿Adónde fue su familia el verano pasado?

_____

II. The other irregular verbs in the preterite fall into a similar pattern. In each, the *yo* form ends in an unstressed *e*; the *él, ella, Ud.* form ends in an unstressed *o*; the other forms have the usual preterite endings. Note the changes in all stems.

Person	hacer	querer	decir	estar	tener	poder	poner
Yo	hice	quise	dije	estuve	tuve	pude	puse
Tú	hiciste	quisiste	dijiste	estuviste	tuviste	pudiste	pusiste
Él, Ella, Ud.	hizo	quiso	dijo	estuvo	tuvo	pudo	puso
Nosotros	hicimos	quisimos	dijimos	estuvimos	tuvimos	pudimos	pusimos
Ellos, Ellas, Uds.	hicieron	quisieron	dijeron	estuvieron	tuvieron	pudieron	pusieron

A. Rewrite the following sentences. Change the verb to the one given in parentheses.

MODELO: ¿Quién hizo esto? (decir) *¿Quién dijo esto?*

1. ¿Quién hizo esto?

   (decir) _____

   (poner) _____

   (querer) _____

2. No hice nada.

   (querer) _____

   (decir) _____

   (tener) _____

3. ¿Los chicos? No, no quisieron.

   (poder) _____

   (decir) _____

   (estar) _____

4. Tuvimos muchas cosas.

   (querer) _____

   (decir) _____

   (hacer) _____

5. ¿Qué tuviste?

(hacer) _____

(querer) _____

(decir) _____

B. Rewrite the following sentences. Change the verbs to agree with each new subject.

MODELO: ¿Qué hice? Pues, quise jugar al tenis pero no pude.

(Paco) *¿Qué hizo? Pues, quiso jugar al tenis pero no pudo.*

1. ¿Qué hice? Pues, quise jugar al tenis pero no pude.

(Tú) _____

(Mi amigo) _____

(Nosotros) _____

2. Paco no tuvo tiempo para comer pero estuvo en el restaurante.

(Mis amigos) _____

(Tú) _____

(Yo) _____

3. Como dijiste, pusiste el libro en el escritorio.

(Mamá) _____

(Los alumnos) _____

(Yo) _____

C. Rewrite the following words in order to form a logical sentence. Change the verb from the infinitive to the preterite form that agrees with the subject. Write each sentence on a piece of notebook paper and then transcribe it below the appropriate illustration on the next page.

MODELO: decir   su   muchas   María   amiga   a   cosas

María dijo muchas cosas a su amiga .

1. en   ¿verdad?   los   tú   platos   mesa   poner   la

2. libro   poder   yo   el   terminar   no

3. yo   tiempo   no   amiga   tener   y   mi

4. hacer   el   ejercicios   muchacho   los

5. en   mis   piscina   amigos   estar   la

6. querer   niño   no   el   estudiar

  MODELO: _María dijo muchas cosas a su amiga_ .

1. _____
_____
_____

2. _____
_____
_____

3. _____
_____
_____

4. _____
_____
_____

5. _____
_____
_____

6. _____
_____
_____

D. *Crucigrama:* Work the crossword puzzle using the preterite tense.

HORIZONTALES

2. (hacer) Ellos _____
3. (querer) Uds. _____
6. (tener) Ellos _____
7. (querer) Pedro _____
9. (poder) Nosotros _____
11. (tener) Tú _____
14. (decir) Tú _____
15. (decir) Ellos _____
19. (ir) Ellos _____
20. (estar) El libro _____
21. (estar) Yo _____
23. (querer) Nosotros _____
25. (ser) Tú _____
29. (poner) Tú _____
30. (estar) Nosotros _____

VERTICALES

1. (ser) Yo _____
2. (hacer) Ud. _____
4. (estar) Tú _____
5. (decir) Ella _____
7. (querer) Yo _____
8. (estar) Los niños _____
10. (hacer) Tú _____
12. (tener) Nosotros _____
13. (poder) Patricia _____
14. (decir) Uds. _____
16. (poder) Yo _____
17. (tener) Pedro _____
18. (poner) Tú y yo _____
19. (ir) Mis amigos y yo _____
22. (hacer) Yo _____
24. (poner) Yo _____
25. (ser) El examen _____
26. (poner) Bárbara _____
27. (tener) Yo _____
28. (decir) Yo _____

Lección III — ¡NO, NO, NO!

GRAMÁTICA: Negative statements, uses of *nunca, nada, nadie, jamás, ningún, ni . . . ni,* and *tampoco*

I.   To make a Spanish statement negative, simply place *no* before the verb.

Juan dijo la verdad.   Juan *no* dijo la verdad.

A.   Rewrite the following sentences. Make each one negative.

MODELO: Anita estudió mucho. <u>Anita no estudió mucho</u>.

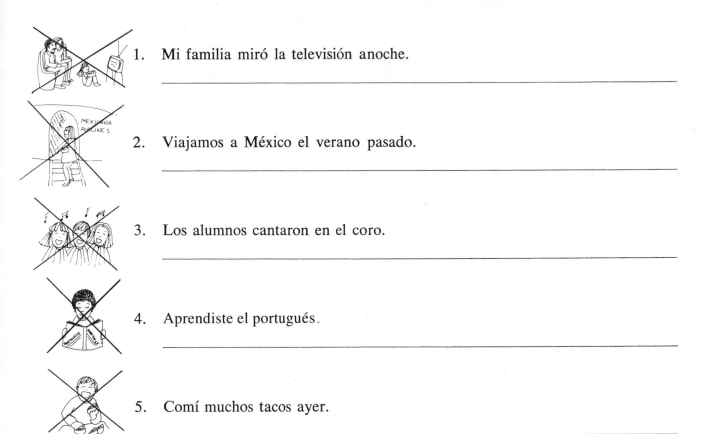

1.   Mi familia miró la televisión anoche.

_____

2.   Viajamos a México el verano pasado.

_____

3.   Los alumnos cantaron en el coro.

_____

4.   Aprendiste el portugués.

_____

5.   Comí muchos tacos ayer.

_____

B.   To answer a question negatively, the double negative is used. *No* is the first word of the answer, followed by a second *no* before the verb.

Answer the following questions in the negative.

MODELO: ¿Viajó Paco a Minnesota? <u>No, Paco no viajó a Minnesota</u>.

1.   ¿Jugaron Uds. al volibol ayer? _____

2.   ¿Tocó la banda en el concierto? _____

3.   ¿Miraste la televisión anoche? _____

4.   ¿Vivieron los chicos en California? _____

5.   ¿Comiste todos los tacos? _____

12

II. In Spanish a double or even a triple negative statement always adds up to a negative.

Common negative words are:

nada - nothing   *nunca* - never
nadie - no one   *jamás* - never   *ningún, (-o)* - not any, none

Note that *ninguno* must agree with the noun it describes and is shortened before a masculine singular noun (*ningún libro*).

A. In the following sentences, write *no* before the verb and the correct negative word in the other blank.

MODELO: ___No___ tengo __nada__. (nothing)

1. Diego _____ dijo _____ a su amigo. (nothing)
2. _____ está _____ en la clase. (no one)
3. _____ hace frío _____ en Acapulco. (never)
4. _____ voy a Rusia _____. (never)
5. El profesor _____ habló con _____. (no one)
6. _____ hay _____ alumna en la clase. (not any)
7. Paco _____ tiene _____ en el escritorio. (nothing)
8. _____ va _____ al partido de fútbol. (no one)
9. _____ hay _____ restaurante bueno. (not any)
10. El Sr. Gómez _____ juega al fútbol _____. (never)

B. Answer the following questions as negatively as you can.

MODELO: ¿Hablaste con tus amigos? _No, no hablé con nadie_.

1. ¿Hay muchas personas en la fiesta? _____
2. ¿Hay un libro en la mesa? _____
3. ¿Fuiste al parque ayer? _____
4. ¿Bailaste con Ana en la fiesta? _____
5. ¿Dijiste el secreto a Mario? _____

III. The Spanish equivalent of *neither . . . nor* is *ni . . . ni*.

Ni Paco ni Juan estudiaron. Neither Paco nor Juan studied.

Combine each pair of sentences to form one sentence using *ni . . . ni*. Change the verb to the plural form.

MODELO: Juan no está en casa. José no está en casa.
Ni Juan ni José están en casa.

1. Mi hermano no sabe nadar. Mi hermana no sabe nadar.

   _____

2. Tomás no fue a la fiesta. José no fue a la fiesta.

   _____

3. María no comió. Ana no comió.

   _____

4. Mamá no tiene tiempo. Papá no tiene tiempo.

   _____

5. Consuelo no habla francés. Paco no habla francés.

   _____

IV. *Tampoco* means *neither* or *not either*.

A. Expand each of the following sentences as in the model.

MODELO: Esta casa no es grande y aquella casa
  no es grande tampoco .

1. Mi hermano no es alto y tu hermano _____
2. Nuestra escuela no es grande y su escuela _____
3. Juanita no es rica y Susana _____
4. La historia no es difícil y el español _____
5. Este libro no es interesante y ese libro _____

B. Answer the following questions using *tampoco*.

MODELO: No quiero ir a clase, ¿y tú?
  No quiero ir a clase tampoco.

1. Paco no va a estudiar, ¿y Alberto?

   _____

2. No tenemos vacaciones ahora, ¿y Uds.?

   _____

3. No me gusta escribir, ¿y tú?

   _____

4. Los chicos no van al partido de fútbol, ¿y las chicas?

   _____

5. El equipo de béisbol no ganó el partido, ¿y el equipo de tenis?

   _____

Lección IV — ¿HACE CUÁNTO TIEMPO?

GRAMÁTICA: *Hacer* in time expressions

I. The English *ago* is expressed in Spanish by *hace* and a period of time.
¿Cuándo fue tu cumpleaños? Hace dos semanas.

A. Match the question on the left with an appropriate answer on the right. Write the questions and answers on the lines below.

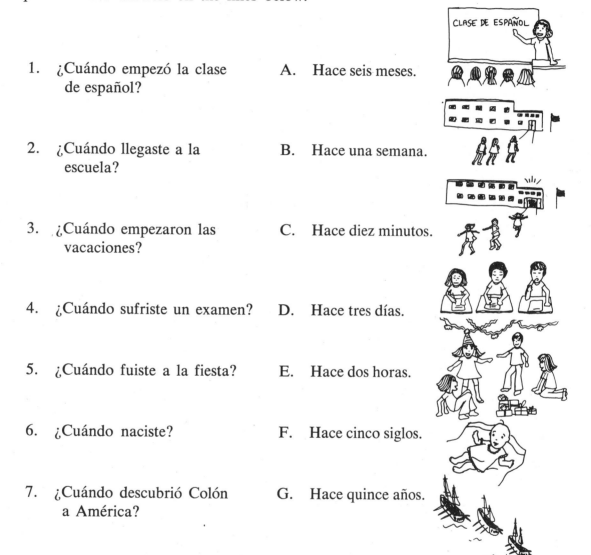

1. ¿Cuándo empezó la clase de español?   A. Hace seis meses.

2. ¿Cuándo llegaste a la escuela?   B. Hace una semana.

3. ¿Cuándo empezaron las vacaciones?   C. Hace diez minutos.

4. ¿Cuándo sufriste un examen?   D. Hace tres días.

5. ¿Cuándo fuiste a la fiesta?   E. Hace dos horas.

6. ¿Cuándo naciste?   F. Hace cinco siglos.

7. ¿Cuándo descubrió Colón a América?   G. Hace quince años.

MODELO: ¿Cuándo fuiste a la fiesta? Hace una semana.

1. _____
2. _____
3. _____
4. _____
5. _____
6. _____

B. Answer the following questions with *hace* and a time expression true for you.

MODELO: ¿Cuándo naciste? _Hace dieciséis años_ .

1. ¿Cuándo se casaron tus padres? _____
2. ¿Cuándo visitaste a tus abuelos? _____
3. ¿Cuándo estuviste enfermo(a)? _____
4. ¿Cuándo naciste? _____
5. ¿Cuándo te levantaste? _____

II. To indicate exactly when some event occurred in the past, use *hace* + (period of time) + *que* + preterite tense verb.

Hace treinta minutos que llegué. I arrived thirty minutes ago.

If the sentence begins with the preterite tense verb, the *que* may be omitted.

Llegué hace treinta minutos.

A. Rewrite the following sentences. Change the word order and omit the *que* as in the example.

MODELO: Hace tres años que viajé a Nueva York.
Viajé a Nueva York hace tres años .

1. Hace veinte años que se casaron mis padres.

   _____

2. Hace tres días que visité a mi amigo.

   _____

3. Hace un mes que fui de compras.

   _____

4. Hace mucho tiempo que jugué al tenis.

   _____

5. Hace diez minutos que llegué a la escuela.

   _____

B. Answer the following questions with time expressions true for you.

MODELO: ¿Cuándo sufriste un examen de inglés?
Hace cuatro días que sufrí un examen de inglés .

1. ¿Cuándo estudiaste para un examen? _____

   _____

2. ¿Cuándo naciste? _____

   _____

3. ¿Cuándo miraste la televisión? _____

   _____

4. ¿Cuándo escuchaste la radio? _____

_____

5. ¿Cuándo jugaste al béisbol? _____

_____

III. To indicate that an action has been going on for a certain period of time use *hace* + (period of time) + *que* + present tense verb.

Hace treinta minutos que estudio. I've been studying for thirty minutes.

If the sentence begins with the present tense verb, the *que* may be omitted.

Estudio hace treinta minutos.

A. Rewrite the following sentences. Change the word order and add the *que* as in the example.

MODELO: Estudio el español hace un año.

Hace un año que estudio el español .

1. Vivo en esta casa hace cinco años.

_____

2. Toco el piano hace cuatro años.

_____

3. Juan es mi amigo hace tres años.

_____

4. Asisto a esta escuela hace un año.

_____

5. Leo este libro hace una hora.

_____

B. Answer the following questions with time expressions true for you.

MODELO: ¿Hace cuánto tiempo que estudias el español?

Hace un año que estudio el español .

1. ¿Hace cuánto tiempo que estudias el español?

_____

2. ¿Hace cuánto tiempo que vives en esta ciudad?

_____

3. ¿Hace cuánto tiempo que asistes a esta escuela?

_____

4. ¿Hace cuánto tiempo que estudias?

_____

5. ¿Hace cuánto tiempo que conoces a tu amigo?

_____

Lección V — EL IMPERFECTO

GRAMÁTICA: Imperfect tense of regular and irregular verbs

I.   In Spanish there are two simple past tenses, the preterite and the imperfect. Look at the examples to see how the imperfect differs from the preterite.

Preterite	Imperfect
Miré la televisión.	*Miraba la televisión.*
I watched television.	I was watching television.
	I used to watch television.

The *preterite* tense is used to indicate that the action was completed. The *imperfect* tense is used to describe what used to happen or to show a repeated or continuing action in the past. To form the imperfect tense of any *-ar* verb, drop the *-ar* and add the following imperfect tense endings.

Person	Ending	Example: hablar — to speak	
Yo	-aba	hablaba	— I was talking, used to talk
Tú	-abas	hablabas	— you were talking, used to talk
Él, Ella, Ud.	-aba	hablaba	— He, she was, you were talking, used to talk
Nosotros	-ábamos	hablábamos	— We were talking, used to talk
Ellos, Ellas, Uds.	-aban	hablaban	— They, you were talking, used to talk

Note that the first and third singular forms are the same and that there is always an accent mark on the *á* of *ábamos*.

A.   Write in the blanks the correct imperfect tense form of the verb given at the top of each list.

MODELO: *estudiar* Yo <u>estudiaba</u>

1.   *escuchar* — to listen

Paco _____

Yo _____

Nosotros _____

Tú _____

Uds. _____

2.   *jugar* — to play a game

Tú _____

Los alumnos _____

Ud. _____

Yo _____

Mis amigos y yo _____

3.   *tocar* — to play an instrument

La profesora _____

Tú y yo _____

Yo _____

Alfredo y Marcos _____

Tú _____

4.   *cantar* — to sing

Mis amigos _____

Yo _____

Tú _____

Ud. y yo _____

Pedro _____

B. Complete the following sentences with the correct imperfect form of the verb in parentheses.

MODELO: (hablar) El profesor _hablaba_ español.

1. (comprar) Mi madre _____ muchas cosas.
2. (preguntar) ¿_____ tú mucho?
3. (ayudar) Mi hermano _____ a mi madre.
4. (visitar) Mis amigos y yo _____ a María.
5. (llegar) Yo _____ tarde a la escuela.
6. (bailar) Mi amigo y yo _____ todos los días.
7. (desear) Yo siempre _____ un perro grande.
8. (trabajar) Mis padres _____ en la oficina.
9. (mirar) ¿_____ tú la televisión?
10. (contestar) El alumno _____ las preguntas.

II. To form the imperfect tense of any *-er* or *-ir* verb, drop the *-er* or *-ir* and add the following imperfect tense endings.

Person	Ending	Example: escribir — to write	
Yo	-ía	escribía	— I used to write, was writing
Tú	-ías	escribías	— You used to write, were writing
Él, Ella, Ud.	-ía	escribía	— He, she, you used to write, was (were) writing
Nosotros	-íamos	escribíamos	— We used to write, were writing
Ellos, Ellas, Uds.	-ían	escribían	— They, you used to write, were writing

Note that the first and third singular forms are the same and that there is an accent mark on the *í* of all the endings.

A. Write in the blanks the correct imperfect tense form of the verb given at the top of each list.

MODELO: *vivir* Yo _vivía_

1. *beber* — to drink
   Yo _____
   Mi amiga _____
   Uds. _____
   Tú _____
   Ud. y yo _____

2. *recibir* — to receive
   Tú _____
   Nosotros _____
   Yo _____
   Marta _____
   Ellas _____

3. *escribir* — to write
   Yo _____
   El alumno _____
   Ellos _____
   Tú _____
   Tú y yo _____

4. *leer* — to read
   Tú _____
   Nosotras _____
   Yo _____
   Mi amigo _____
   Los niños _____

B. Complete the following sentences with the correct imperfect form of the verb given at the top of each list.

MODELO: *comer*   Anita siempre _comía_ mucho.

1. *comer*

   a. Yo siempre _____ mucho.

   b. Pedro siempre _____ mucho.

   c. Los chicos siempre _____ mucho.

   d. Tú siempre _____ mucho.

   e. Mis amigos y yo siempre _____ mucho.

2. *decir*

   a. Paco siempre _____ la verdad.

   b. Yo siempre _____ la verdad.

   c. Tú siempre _____ la verdad.

   d. Los profesores siempre _____ la verdad.

   e. Mi amigo y yo siempre _____ la verdad.

III. Only three Spanish verbs are irregular in the imperfect tense: *ir*, *ser*, and *ver*.

Person	*ir* — to go	*ser* — to be	*ver* — to see
Yo	iba	era	veía
Tú	ibas	eras	veías
Él, Ella, Ud.	iba	era	veía
Nosotros	íbamos	éramos	veíamos
Ellos, Ellas, Uds.	iban	eran	veían

A. Complete the following sentences with the correct imperfect form of the verb given at the top of each list.

MODELO: *ir*   Yo _iba_ al cine todos los sábados.

1. *ir*

   a. Yo _____ al parque todos los días.

   b. Mis amigos _____ al parque todos los días.

   c. Nosotros _____ al parque todos los días.

   d. Tú _____ al parque todos los días.

   e. Pedro _____ al parque todos los días.

2. *ser*

   a. Yo _____ rico.

   b. Ud. _____ rico.

   c. Nosotros _____ ricos.

   d. Tú _____ rico.

   e. Uds. _____ ricos.

3. *ver*

    a. Tú _____ a tus amigos todo el tiempo.

    b. Ud. _____ a sus amigos todo el tiempo.

    c. Yo _____ a mis amigos todo el tiempo.

    d. Ana y yo _____ a nuestros amigos todo el tiempo.

    e. Los jóvenes _____ a sus amigos todo el tiempo.

B. Rewrite the following sentences. Change the verb forms and the word *joven* to agree with each new subject.

MODELO: Cuando era joven, Paco siempre iba al cine y veía las películas.

(Uds.) *Cuando eran jóvenes, Uds. siempre iban al cine y veían las películas* .

1. (Yo) _____

    _____

2. (María) _____

    _____

3. (Uds.) _____

    _____

4. (Nosotros) _____

    _____

5. (Tú) _____

    _____

IV. A. Answer the following questions with responses true for you.

MODELO: ¿Hacía frío durante el invierno? *Sí, hacía frío.*

1. ¿Conocías al profesor de español?

    _____

2. ¿Siempre podías jugar al tenis?

    _____

3. ¿Iban Uds. al campo todos los veranos?

    _____

4. ¿Te gustaba la escuela?

    _____

5. ¿Estabas enfermo cuando eras niño?

    _____

B. Write a paragraph describing your life when you were younger.

Use at least five of the following expressions:

Cuando yo tenía _____ años . . .   Mi familia vivía . . .
Me gustaba jugar a . . .   Jugaba con . . .
Mi(s) amigo(s) era(n) . . .   No me gustaba . . .
Me gustaba mucho . . .   Siempre iba a . . .
Quería . . .   No podía . . .
Mi casa estaba en . . .   Viajábamos a . . .

_____
_____
_____
_____
_____

C. Now write a paragraph describing the life of a friend when he or she was younger. Use at least five expressions in the imperfect. Refer to the list in part B for help. Change the verb and other forms as necessary.

_____
_____
_____
_____
_____

Lección VI — ¿IMPERFECTO O PRETÉRITO?

GRAMÁTICA: Comparison of uses of preterite and imperfect tenses

I. You have learned that in Spanish both the imperfect and preterite tenses are used to express action in the past. The *preterite* is used to indicate that the action was completed. The *imperfect* tense is used to describe what used to happen or to show a repeated or continuing action in the past. If you wish to tell about an action that was going on when something else happened, both the preterite and the imperfect tense are used.

> Mientras *comía, sonó* el teléfono.
> While I was eating, the telephone rang.

The *imperfect* tense is used for the action that was going on when something else happened. The *preterite* tense is used for the completed action, the action that interrupted what was going on.

A. Match each phrase in List A with any logical phrase in List B. Copy the entire sentence on the lines below. There is more than one correct answer.

List A

1. Mientras Juan estudiaba,
2. Mientras yo comía,
3. Mientras papá leía,
4. Mientras hablábamos por teléfono,
5. Mientras miraba la televisión,
6. Mientras mis amigos jugaban al tenis,

List B

A. mi mamá entró.
B. su amigo llamó.
C. mi hermanito gritó.
D. Pacó llegó a la casa.

E. entré a la sala.
F. Pedro salió del parque.

MODELO: <u>Mientras Juan estudiaba, Paco llegó a la casa</u> .

1. _____
2. _____
3. _____
4. _____
5. _____

B. Fill in the blanks below with the correct preterite and imperfect verb forms. The following infinitives will help you: *estudiar, comer, leer, hablar, escribir, abrir, cerrar, llegar, interrumpir, entrar, sonar, gritar, llamar.*

MODELO: Yo <u>leía</u> cuando Juan <u>llegó</u> .
        (was reading)   (arrived)

1. María _____ por teléfono cuando yo _____ .
      (was talking)   (arrived)

2. Mis amigos _____ cuando el profesor _____ .
      (were studying)   (entered)

3. ¿ _____ tú cuando yo _____ por teléfono?
   (Were you sleeping)   (called)

4. _____ el teléfono mientras mi familia y yo _____ .
   (Rang)   (were eating)

5. La clase _____ cuando la profesora _____ .
   (was reading)   (interrupted)

6. Yo _____ cuando mi hermanito _____ el libro.
   (was reading)   (closed)

7. El profesor _____ las ventanas mientras nosotros _____ .
   (opened)   (were writing)

8. Las niñas _____ mientras nosotros _____ .
   (shouted)   (were studying)

9. Yo _____ cuando _____ el teléfono.
   (was sleeping)   (rang)

10. Mientras nosotros _____ mi mamá _____ la puerta.
    (were talking)   (closed)

C. Answer each of the following questions in the imperfect tense. The sketch to the right of each question will help you select your answer.

estudiaba   **jugaba al tenis**   **hablaba con mis amigos**

comía   **dormía**

MODELO: ¿Qué hacías cuando Paco llamó por teléfono?

Jugaba al tenis cuando Paco llamó por teléfono .

1. ¿Qué hacías cuando llegó el profesor?

   _____

   _____

2. ¿Qué hacías cuando sonó el teléfono?

   _____

   _____

3. ¿Qué hacías cuando entró mamá?

_____

_____

4. ¿Qué hacías cuando empezó a llover?

_____

_____

5. ¿Qué hacías cuando llamó José?

_____

_____

D. Hidden in the maze below are five verbs in the imperfect tense and five in the preterite. Find and circle each, then fill in the blanks in the sentences with the correct verb.

Preterite	*Imperfect*
interrumpí	hablaba
saliste	estudiabas
llegó	comía
entramos	mirábamos
llegaron	dormían

```
a  s  a  l  i  s  t  e  t  g  a  a
n  o  r  a  g  e  ll s  m  o  b  j
m  m  b  o  d  n  e  v  b  f  a  o
a  a  í  a  m  t  r  a  m  c  ó  o
b  b  b  a  ó  r  q  t  d  t  o  g
a  á  s  a  b  a  i  d  u  t  s  e
l  r  n  a  í  m  r  o  d  a  a  ll
b  i  a  í  m  o  c  r  m  s  l  j
a  m  a  t  z  s  s  o  o  í  a  m
h  e  a  í  p  m  u  rr e  t  n  i
```

1. Yo __comía__ cuando _____ Paco.
2. Tú _____ cuando nosotros _____ .
3. Mientras Paco _____ , yo _____ .
4. Mientras nosotros _____ , las niñas _____ .
5. Mientras todos _____ , tú _____ .

Lección VII — HAY Y HABÍA

GRAMÁTICA: *Hay* and *Había*; use with numbers to 1,000,000

I.   The single word *hay* means there is or there are.
Había is the same word in the past. It means there was or there were.

Hay muchos alumnos en la clase. There are many students in the class.

Había mucha gente allí. There were many people there.

A.   Make up sentences using *hay* and *había*. Use the word pair given for each exercise.
Write one sentence in the present tense, then write the same sentence in the past.

MODELO: un libro - la mesa   Hay un libro en la mesa   .
Había un libro en la mesa   .

1.   muchas personas - la piscina
_____
_____

2.   muchos animales - el parque zoológico
_____
_____

3.   una piñata - la fiesta
_____
_____

4.   un hombre grande - la bicicleta
_____
_____

5.   tiburones - el océano
_____
_____
_____

B.   Answer the following questions with responses true for you.

MODELO: ¿Hay diez personas en tu familia?
No, no hay diez personas en mi familia   .

1.   ¿Hay cinco personas en tu familia?
_____

26

2. ¿Hay un perro en tu casa?

_____

3. ¿Hay muchos alumnos inteligentes en la clase?

_____

4. ¿Había un examen la semana pasada?

_____

5. ¿Había muchos días de vacaciones el año pasado?

_____

II. Once you have learned Spanish numbers to 100, the rest are easy.

100 - ciento	600 - seiscientos
200 - doscientos	700 - setecientos
300 - trescientos	800 - ochocientos
400 - cuatrocientos	900 - novecientos
500 - quinientos	

Ciento is shortened to *cien* before a noun it describes.

    cien personas - 100 people   *cien* dólares - $100

Numbers in the hundreds, with the exception of *ciento,* must have masculine or feminine endings.

    quininent*as* alumn*as* - 500 (girl) students
    seiscient*os* alumn*os* - 600 (boy) students

A. Rewrite the following sentences. Replace the numeral with the correct word.

    MODELO: Hay 800 alumnos en la escuela.

      Hay ochocientos alumnos en la escuela .

1. Hay 900 libros en la biblioteca.

_____

2. Hay 100 preguntas en el examen.

_____

3. Hay 300 alumnas en la cafetería.

_____

4. Había 700 personas en el partido de fútbol.

_____

5. Había 500 chicos en el baile.

_____

B. *Mil* means 1.000. The word *un* is never used before *mil.*

    mil - 1.000   dos mil - 2.000   tres mil - 3.000

In Spanish, numbers above 900 may not be counted in hundreds as we sometimes do in English.

Mil cuatrocientos libros   Fourteen hundred books

Millón means 1.000.000. The article *un* must be used when speaking of a million. *Millón* has a plural form, *millones*. If a noun immediately follows *millón* or *millones*, you must use the word *de* between it and the noun.

1.000.000 libros - un millón de libros
2.200.000 libros - dos millones doscientos mil libros

Note: In Spanish punctuation, a period rather than a comma separates thousands from hundreds.

Write the following phrases using correct Spanish words.

MODELO: 2.000 casas ___dos mil casas_____

1.   2.800 coches _____
2.   2.200.00 casas _____
3.   3.900 pesos _____
4.   7.300 años _____
5.   4.700 dólares _____
6.   7.500 libros _____
7.   1.000 habitantes _____
8.   8.200 personas _____
9.   1.000.000 pesetas _____
10. 5.600 alumnos _____

C.   A year in Spanish is always expressed as *mil novecientos setenta y ocho*, not as nineteen seventy-eight as we do in English. Write the year which correctly answers each question.

MODELO: ¿En qué año nació tu papá? _Mil novecientos cuarenta_
_y dos_____

1.   ¿En qué año nació tu papá? _____
2.   ¿En qué año entraste en esta escuela? _____
_____
3.   ¿En qué año naciste tú? _____
4.   ¿En qué año descubrió Colón a América? _____
_____
5.   ¿En qué año estamos? _____

Lección VIII — ME, TE, NOS, LO, LOS

GRAMÁTICA: Direct object pronouns

I. Object pronouns receive the action of a verb. A *direct object* pronoun receives the action directly. (He hit *me*.) In Spanish, *me*, *te*, and *nos* are three object pronouns. They come right before the verb.

Miguel *me* visita.	Miguel visits me.
La profesora *te* mira.	The teacher looks at you.
Pepe *nos* ayuda.	Pepe helps us.

A. Rewrite the following sentences. Place the direct object pronoun before the verb.

MODELO: (me) Carlos ayuda. _Carlos me ayuda_ .

1. (nos) Mi madre ve. _____

2. (me) Ellos visitan. _____

3. (te) Yo ayudo. _____

4. (nos) Nuestros amigos ayudan. _____

5. (te) Pedro ve. _____

B. In each section, write three different sentences. Use the subject and verb you are given and combine them with *me*, *te*, and *nos*. Write the English meaning of each sentence.

MODELO: Juan ayuda.

Juan me ayuda.	_Juan helps me._
Juan te ayuda.	_Juan helps you._
Juan nos ayuda.	_Juan helps us._

1. Mi madre mira.

_____   _____

_____   _____

_____   _____

2. Mis amigos ayudan.

_____   _____

_____   _____

_____   _____

3. Susana visita.

_____   _____

_____   _____

_____   _____

C. Answer the following questions. Use the direct object pronoun given.

MODELO: ¿A quién visitan los amigos? (Me) _Me visitan_ .

1. ¿A quién mira el profesor?

   (te) _____

2. ¿A quiénes ayuda Marta?

   (nos) _____

3. ¿A quiénes invitan los amigos?

   (nos) _____

4. ¿A quién mira Juan?

   (me) _____

5. ¿A quién visita José?

   (te) _____

II. *Lo* and *los* and *la* and *las* are used as direct object pronouns in the same way that *me*, *te*, and *nos* are used.

lo - you (masc.), him, it   la - you (fem.), her, it
los - you (masc. pl.), them (masc.)   las - you (fem. pl.), them (fem.)

Carlos *lo* mira.   Carlos looks at him (you, it).

A. Rewrite the following sentences. Replace the underlined noun object with the correct pronoun (*lo, la, los,* or *las*).

MODELO: Juan tiene el libro. _Juan lo tiene_ .

1. Tenemos las plumas. _____
2. El profesor cierra el libro. _____
3. Paco quiere a Susana. _____
4. Conozco a los jugadores. _____
5. Miguel invita a Juan. _____
6. Encontré a Ud. (fem.) _____
7. Busco a Ud. (masc.) _____
8. Veo a Uds. (masc.) _____
9. Papá mira la televisión. _____
10. Invitamos a Susana y Teresa. _____

B. Complete the following sentences using the model as a guide. Write the correct direct object pronoun as well as the proper verb form.

MODELO: No entiendo la lección pero Juan _la entiende_ .

1. Carmen no invita a Pablo pero Susana _____
2. No tengo los papeles pero mi amigo _____

3. María no conoce a las chicas pero Anita _____

4. No visito a mi amiga pero Pedro _____

5. No cierro la puerta pero Ud. _____

6. Mi madre no conoce a Ud. (masc.) pero mi padre _____

7. Yo no invito a Uds. (masc.) pero mi amigo _____

8. No como el plátano pero mi hermana _____

9. No busco a Ud. (fem.) pero mi amigo _____

10. No leo las lecciones pero Antonio _____

C. Answer the following questions using only the correct verb form and the direct object pronoun.

MODELO: ¿Tienes el libro? __Lo tengo_____ .

1. ¿Visitas a Paco? _____

2. ¿Entiendes el francés? _____

3. ¿Escribes los ejercicios? _____

4. ¿Ve Paco a Juan? _____

5. ¿Tienes todos los libros? _____

6. ¿Invita Eduardo a Patricia? _____

7. ¿Escuchas a tu mamá? _____

8. ¿Conoce Juan a los niños? _____

9. ¿Miras la televisión? _____

10. ¿Tiene el profesor la tiza? _____

III. Direct object pronouns are attached to the end of the verb when they are used with an infinitive.

¿Vas a comprar el vestido? Sí, voy a comprar*lo*.
¿Tienes que comprar el libro? Sí, tengo que comprar*lo*.

Rewrite the following sentences. Replace the underlined noun object with the correct pronoun.

MODELO: Voy a ayudar a mamá. __Voy a ayudarla_____ .

1. Tengo que visitar a ti. _____

2. Paco quiere ayudar a nosotros. _____

3. Mis padres pueden visitar a mí. _____

4. Pedro quiere invitar a Susana. _____

5. Tengo que leer los libros. _____

Lección IX — ME, TE, NOS, LE, LES

GRAMÁTICA: Indirect object pronouns; use of indirect object pronouns with direct object pronouns

I.   You have learned to use *me*, *te*, and *nos* as direct object pronouns. The same words may be also used as *indirect* object pronouns. An indirect object tells *to whom* or *for whom* something is done. The word *to* or *for* may be expressed or implied in the English translation. In Spanish, indirect object pronouns are placed before the verb.

Juan *me* dice la verdad. John tells (to) me the truth.

A.   Rewrite the following sentences. Place the indirect object pronoun before the verb. Then write the English meaning of each sentence.

MODELO: (me) Mi amigo da un regalo.

Mi amigo me da un regalo. My friend gives me a gift.

1. (te) Paco da un regalo.

_____

2. (nos) El profesor explica la lección.

_____

3. (me) Tú escribes mucho.

_____

4. (te) Yo siempre digo la verdad.

_____

5. (nos) La profesora habla en español.

_____

B.   Answer the following questions. Replace the underlined phrase with the pronoun given and change word order as necessary.

MODELO: ¿A quién escribe Juan una carta?

(te) Juan te escribe una carta .

1. ¿A quién da mamá los regalos?
    (nos) _____

2. ¿A quién habla el profesor?
    (me) _____

3. ¿A quién explica la lección el profesor?
    (te) _____

4. ¿A quién escriben los amigos?
    (nos) _____

5. ¿Para quién compra papá helado?
    (me) _____

32

II. The other indirect object pronouns are different from direct object pronouns. *Le* means (to or for) you, him, or her. *Les* means (to or for) you (pl.) or them.

    Juan *le* dice la verdad.   John tells (to) him (her, you) the truth.
    Juan *les* dice la verdad.   John tells (to) them (you, pl.) the truth.

Since the same words are used for both masculine and feminine objects, it is sometimes necessary to add phrases like *a Ud.*, *a él*, or *a ella*, in order to make the meaning of a sentence clear.

    Le dice la verdad *a Ud.*   He tells (to) you the truth.
    Les dice la verdad *a ellas.*   He tells (to) them the truth.

A.   Fill in each blank with *le* or *les*.

MODELO: __Le__ escribo una carta. (a Ud.)

1. _____ dice la verdad. (a ellos)
2. _____ explica la lección. (a él)
3. El profesor _____ habla. (a Paco)
4. Ellos _____ cantan. (a Uds.)
5. Los chicos _____ dan una serenata. (a María)
6. ¿Quién _____ escribió una carta? (a Ud.)
7. El hombre _____ enseña el coche nuevo. (a los chicos)
8. Mi mamá _____ sirve la comida. (a ella)
9. _____ compré un regalo. (a ellas)
10. _____ hacemos una fiesta. (a las chicas)

B.   Rewrite the following sentences with the correct pronoun: *me, te, nos, le,* or *les*.

MODELO: Paco dice la verdad. (a Susana.) _Paco le dice la verdad_ .

1. El profesor explica la lección. (a nosotros.)

    _____

2. Mi mamá sirve la comida. (a Susana.)

    _____

3. El profesor da muchos libros. (a los alumnos.)

    _____

4. Escribí una carta. (a ti.)

    _____

5. Miguel pasa el pan. (a mí.)

    _____

C. Answer the following questions. Be careful. Sometimes it is necessary to change the verb form and/or the indirect object pronoun in your answer.

MODELO: ¿Me compraste una blusa?

Sí, te compré una blusa .

1. ¿Me escribiste una carta?

_____

2. ¿Les hablaste por teléfono?

_____

3. ¿Nos dijiste la verdad?

_____

4. ¿Te escribió Juan?

_____

5. ¿Le compraste un regalo?

_____

III. If you wish to say something like "He explains it to me," it is necessary to use two pronouns, one direct and one indirect. The *indirect* object pronoun will come before the direct object pronoun.

Juan *me* lo da.   John gives it to me.
Juan *nos* los da.   John gives them to us.

The pronoun referring to a person always comes first. In order to avoid an awkward *le-lo* or *les-los* combination, *se* is used in place of either *le* or *les* whenever the two pronouns are used together. It may be necessary to add phrases like *a. Ud., a él,* or *a ella* for clarity.

Juan *se* lo da.   John gives it to him.

A. In the following sentences, circle the direct object and underline the indirect object.

MODELO: Paco les da (los libros) a Uds.

1. Paco le da el libro a Juan.
2. Paco les da la pluma a Uds.
3. Paco les da los libros a Juan y a Pedro.
4. Paco le da las plumas a Juan.
5. Paco te da el libro a ti.
6. Paco te da las plumas a ti.
7. Paco me da los libros a mí.
8. Paco me da la pluma a mí.
9. Paco nos da los libros a nostros.
10. Paco nos da la pluma a nosotras.

B. Now match each sentence in part A with its shortened form below. Write the *number* of the sentence from part A next to the sentence below.

1. Nos los da. _____
2. Me la da. _____
3. Nos la da. _____
4. Se los da. _____
5. Me los da. _____

6. Se lo da. _____
7. Se la da. _____
8. Se los da. _____
9. Te lo da. _____
10. Se las da. _____
11. Te las da. _____

C. Rewrite the following sentences. Replace both the direct and indirect objects with the correct pronouns.

MODELO: El profesor le explica la lección a Paco.
El profesor se la explica .

1. Mi mamá les sirve la comida a mis amigos.
   _____

2. Alberto le compró regalos.
   _____

3. Mi padre me enseñó el coche.
   _____

4. El Sr. Gómez nos escribió cartas.
   _____

5. Te compré un regalo.
   _____

D. Answer the following questions. Change the verb form as necessary and use both direct and indirect object pronouns in place of the nouns.

MODELO: ¿Me compraste una blusa? _Sí, te la compré_ .

1. ¿Le escribiste una carta a Paco? _____
2. ¿Me dijiste la verdad? _____
3. ¿Nos escribió Juan una carta? _____
4. ¿Te compró mamá un regalo? _____
5. ¿Les explicó el profesor las lecciones a los alumnos?
   _____
6. ¿Me mandaste las flores? _____
7. ¿Compraste los regalos para tus padres? _____
8. ¿Le enseñó el Sr. Gómez el coche a tu papá? _____
9. ¿Compraste el libro para mí? _____
10. ¿Te escribió Paco cartas? _____

IV. When used with an infinitive, both direct and indirect object pronouns are attached to the verb.

> Voy a escribir*te* una carta.

When two object pronouns are used, both are attached.

> Voy a escribirte una carta. Voy a escribír*tela*.

Note: An accent must be added when two pronouns are attached to the infinitive.

Rewrite the following sentences. Replace both objects with the correct pronouns and place them after the verb.

MODELO: Voy a comprarte una blusa. _Voy a comprártela_.

1. Tengo que escribirle una carta a Paco. _____
2. ¿Vas a decirme la verdad? _____
3. Juan quiere escribirnos una carta? _____
4. Mamá va a comprarte un regalo. _____
5. El profesor quiere explicarles las lecciones a los alumnos.

_____

Lección X — MÁS PRONOMBRES

GRAMÁTICA: Pronouns after prepositions

I. The Spanish pronouns used after prepositions are exactly like the subject pronouns (*él*, *ella*, *Ud.*, *nosotros*, *nosotras*, *ellos*, *ellas*, *Uds.*) except for *mí* (me) and *ti* (you, fam.).

mí	La invitación es para *mí*.	The invitation is for me.
ti	Hablan de *ti*.	They talk about you.
él	Voy con *él*.	I'm going with him.

Replace the words in parentheses with the proper pronoun.

MODELO: La carta es para _mí_____ (yo).

1. No es para _____ (tú).

2. Recibí un regalo de _____ (Uds.).

3. Voy con _____ (Ud.).

4. Esta casa es de _____ (Juan y yo).

5. No pienso en _____ (ella).

6. Hablamos con _____ (Pedro y Paco).

7. ¿Tienes algo para _____ (yo)?

8. Creemos en _____ (tú).

9. La invitación es de _____ (yo).

10. Estudio con _____ (mis amigos).

II. After the preposition *con*, *mí* and *ti* become *conmigo* and *contigo*. All other forms remain the same.

Juan habla *conmigo*.   John talks with me.
Voy *contigo*.   I'm going with you.

A. Rewrite the following sentences. Replace the underlined word with the proper pronoun.

MODELO: Juan va con Ud. (yo) _Juan va conmigo_____ .

1. Juan va con Ud.

   a. (ella) _____

   b. (Uds.) _____

   c. (yo) _____

   d. (nosotros) _____

   e. (tú) _____

2. El profesor habla con nosotras.

   a. (ellos) _____

   b. (yo) _____

c. (Ud.) _____

d. (Uds.) _____

e. (tú) _____

B. Rewrite the following sentences. Replace the underlined words with the proper pronouns.

MODELO: Es la casa de Juan y Pedro. Es la casa de _ellos_____.

1. Hablé por teléfono con Bárbara.

   _____

2. Voy a estudiar con _____ (tú).

   _____

3. ¿Tienes algo para Graciela y yo?

   _____

4. La carta es de Alicia y Marta.

   _____

5. ¿Vas a la escuela con _____ (yo)?

   _____

Lección XI — LAS COMPARACIONES

GRAMÁTICA: Comparison of adjectives: *más (menos) que*; *el (la) más (menos) — de*;
mejor-peor, mayor-menor

I.   In English, we often compare one person or thing by adding *-er* or *-est* to an adjective.
In Spanish, the word *más* or the article (*el* or *la*) plus *más* is placed before the adjective.

Juan es alto.	John is tall.
Pedro es *más* alto.	Peter is taller.
José es *el más* alto.	Joe is the tallest.
Carmen es guapa.	Carmen is pretty.
Susana es *más* guapa.	Susan is prettier.
Elena es *la más* guapa.	Ellen is the prettiest.

A.   Write three comparative statements about people you know. Use the adjective given
and any names you wish.

MODELO: (guapo)   _Alberto es guapo_ .
Miguel es más guapo .
José es el más guapo .

1.   (inteligente) _____
_____
_____

2.   (perezozo, -a) _____
_____
_____

39

3. (fuerte) _____

_____

_____

4. (guapo, -a) _____

_____

_____

5. (alto, -a) _____

_____

_____

B. In order to express the idea of less than or least, *menos* or *el* (*la*) *menos* is used in the same way as *más*.

Juan no es alto.   John is not tall.

José es *menos* alto.   Joe is less tall.

Jaime es *el menos* alto.   Jim is the least tall.

Write two comparative sentences based on the sentence given. Change the underlined words to appropriate words of your choice.

MODELO: La casa de <u>Miguel</u> no es grande. *La casa de Anita es menos grande. La casa del Sr. Gómez es la menos grande.*

1. La clase de <u>español</u> no es difícil.

_____

_____

2. La silla <u>roja</u> no es cómoda.

_____

_____

3. El libro de <u>matemáticas</u> no es interesante.

_____

_____

4. <u>Massachusetts</u> no es grande.

_____

_____

40

5. La naranja no es deliciosa.

_____

_____

C. To say that something is the most ___ or least ___ of a group, the expression *el (la) más (menos) ___ de ___* is used.

Juan es *el más alto de* la clase. John is the tallest in the class.

Esta clase es *la menos difícil de* la escuela. This class is the least difficult in the school.

Complete the following sentences with the proper comparative phrase. The following adjectives will help you: *bonito, interesante, inteligente, grande, alto.*

MODELO: Beto es ___*el más alto de*___ la clase.
                          (the tallest in)

1. María es _____ su familia.
              (the prettiest in)

2. Este libro es _____ la biblioteca.
                  (the most interesting in)

3. El vestido es _____ la tienda.
                  (the least big in)

4. Margarita es _____ esta clase.
                 (the most intelligent in)

5. Alfredo es _____ su familia.
               (the least tall in)

D. Complete each statement with the appropriate phrase using *el (la) más ___ de todos.*

MODELO: Este melón es delicioso pero ese melón *es el más*
        ___*delicioso de todos*___ .

1. Texas es grande pero Alaska _____

2. El Misisipí es largo pero el Nilo _____

3. Anita es lista pero Susana _____

4. Tu casa es moderna pero mi casa _____

5. Alberto es inteligente pero Juanita _____

E. Answer each question with a response true for you.

MODELO: ¿Cuál es la clase más difícil este año?
        ___*Inglés es la clase más difícil*___ .

41

1. ¿Cuál es el estado más bonito de los Estados Unidos?

   _____

2. ¿Cuál es la actriz (el actor) más guapa(-o) del cine?

   _____

3. ¿Cuál es el programa más interesante de la televisión?

   _____

4. ¿Cuál es la clase más fácil de la escuela?

   _____

5. ¿Cuál es el deporte más interesante?

   _____

II. Special words are used in Spanish for *better-best*, *worse-worst*, *younger-youngest*, and *older-oldest*.

mejor (better, best)	peor (worse, worst)
menor (younger, youngest)	mayor (older, oldest)

La escuela Kennedy es buena.	Kennedy School is good.
La escuela Johnson es *mejor*.	Johnson School is better.
La escuela Taft es *la mejor* de todas.	Taft School is the best of all.

A. Complete the following sentences with the proper comparative expressions.

   MODELO: Este libro es bueno.
   Ese libro es ___*mejor*___ . (better)
   Aquel libro es *el mejor de todos* . (best of all)

   1. Este coche es malo.

      Ese coche es _____ . (worse)

      Aquel coche es _____ . (worst of all)

   2. Paco es joven.

      Pedro es _____ . (younger)

      Elena es _____ . (youngest of all)

   3. El Sr. Guzmán es viejo.

      La Sra. Martín es_____ . (older)

      La Srta. Rodríguez es _____ . (oldest of all)

   4. La escuela de Pedro es buena.

      Tu escuela es _____ . (better)

      Mi escuela es _____ . (best of all)

B. Answer the following questions with responses true for you.

MODELO: ¿Quién es el menor de tu familia?

Susan es la menor .

1. ¿Quién es el menor de tu familia?

_____

2. ¿Quién es el mayor de tu familia?

_____

3. ¿Cuál es el mejor programa de televisión?

_____

4. ¿Cuál es el peor programa de televisión?

_____

5. ¿Cuál es la mejor clase que tienes?

_____

III. To express the idea of more than or less (fewer) than a numeral, the phrases _más de_ or _menos de_ are used.

Tengo _más de treinta_ dólares.   I have more than $30.
Hay _menos de 40_ alumnos en la clase.   There are fewer than forty students in the class.

A. Complete each sentence with a _más de_ expression.

MODELO: Paco tiene doce años pero yo _tengo más de doce años_ .

1. Mis padres tienen tres hijos pero mis tíos tienen

_____

2. Felipe tiene seis clases pero yo tengo

_____

3. El Sr. Guzmán tiene cien libros pero la Sra. Guzmán tiene

_____

4. Mi amigo tiene catorce años pero yo tengo

_____

B. Rewrite the sentences in part A using the appropriate _menos de_ expression.

MODELO: Paco tiene doce años pero yo tengo _menos de doce años_ .

1. _____

2. _____

3. _____

4. _____

_____

C. Answer the following questions. Use *más de* or *menos de* in a response true for you.

MODELO: ¿Tienes tres hermanos? *No, tengo menos de tres*
hermanos _____.

1. ¿Tienes tres hermanos? _____

2. ¿Tienes cien dólares? _____

3. ¿Tienes diez amigos? _____

4. ¿Tienes ocho clases? _____

5. ¿Tienes dos perros? _____

IV. When not using a numeral in comparison, the idea of *more . . . than* is expressed *más*
_____ *que.* Less *. . . than* is *menos* _____ *que.*

Paco es *más inteligente que* Alfredo.
Esta clase es *menos grande que* esa clase.

Better than and *worse than* are expressed *mejor que* and *peor que.*

Esta escuela es *mejor que* la otra escuela.
Este libro es *peor que* el otro libro.

Older than and *younger than* are *mayor que* and *menor que.*

Susana es *mayor que* Alicia.
Mi hermano es *menor que* mi hermana.

A. Fill in the blanks with the appropriate comparative phrase: *mejor que, peor que,
mayor que, menor que, más . . . que, menos . . . que.*

MODELO: Pablo es _____ *más alto que* _____ Alfredo.
(more tall than)

1. Pizza es _____ chop suey.
(more delicious than)

2. California es _____ Alaska.
(less big than)

3. Nuestro equipo de béisbol es _____ el equipo de fútbol.
(better than)

4. Mi examen es _____ tu examen.
(worse than)

5. Mi hermano es _____ yo.
(younger than)

6. Yo soy _____ mi hermano.
(older than)

7. El libro de inglés es _____ el libro de historia.
(more interesting than)

8. Chicago es _____ St. Louis.
   (bigger than)

9. La televisión es _____ la radio.
   (better than)

10. El profesor es _____ sus alumnos.
    (older than)

B. Write a comparative sentence using *que* to answer each question.

MODELO: ¿Cuál es mejor: pizza o chop suey?

 Chop suey es mejor que pizza .

1. ¿Cuál es mejor: un coche o una motocicleta?

   _____

2. ¿Cuál es peor: un examen de español o un examen de inglés?

   _____

3. ¿Quién es mayor: tu abuelo o tu papá?

   _____

4. ¿Quién es menor: el profesor de inglés o el profesor de español?

   _____

5. ¿Cuál es más grande: tu casa o la de tu amigo?

   _____

6. ¿Cuál es menos caro: un coche o una bicicleta?

   _____

7. ¿Cuál es más grande: Nueva York o Chicago?

   _____

8. ¿Cuál es más interesante: un libro o una película?

   _____

9. ¿Cuál es mejor: estudiar o jugar?

   _____

10. ¿Cuál es más delicioso: pizza o chop suey?

    _____

Lección XII — BUEN, MAL, PRIMER, TERCER, GRAN

GRAMÁTICA: Shortened adjectives

I. When used before a masculine singular noun, four Spanish adjectives are shortened by dropping the ending -o.

un *buen* libro — a good book   el *mal* tiempo — the bad weather
el *primer* día — the first day   el *tercer* año — the third year

In all other situations, the adjective must agree in number and gender with the noun.

un libro *malo*   la *tercera* clase
los *primeros* alumnos   las *malas* plumas

A. Write the shortened form of the adjectives given.

MODELO: (primero) el __*primer*__ día

1. (bueno) el _____ hombre
2. (primero) el _____ alumno
3. (tercero) el _____ examen
4. (malo) el _____ libro
5. (bueno) el _____ profesor

B. Answer the questions using the shortened form of the adjective.

MODELO: ¿Es el Sr. Gómez un profesor bueno?

__Sí, es un buen profesor_____ .

1. ¿Es la fiesta el sábado tercero de mayo?

   _____

2. ¿Es José un capitán bueno?

   _____

3. ¿Es el martes el día primero de la escuela?

   _____

4. ¿Es un examen malo? _____

5. ¿Es Paquito un niño bueno? _____

C. Write the correct form of the adjective given.

MODELO: (bueno) Es una __*buena*__ profesora.

1. (malo) El bandido es un _____ hombre.
2. (bueno) El Sr. Guzmán es un _____ profesor.
3. (malo) Margarita y Lupe no son _____ chicas.
4. (primero) Vamos durante los _____ días de junio.
5. (malo) Esta no es una _____ clase.

6. (tercero) ¿Cuántas alumnas hay en la _____ fila?

7. (primero) La _____ lección es fácil.

8. (bueno) ¿Es un _____ libro?

9. (tercero) Miércoles es el _____ día de la semana.

10. (malo) La escuela tiene un _____ equipo de fútbol.

II. The word *grande* means large when it appears *after* a noun. It has two forms, *grande* (singular) and *grandes* (plural).

El hombre es *grande*.

The man is big.

Las naciones son *grandes*.

The countries are big.

When *grande* comes before a noun it has two forms: *gran* (singular) and *grandes* (plural). The meaning changes to great when used *before* a noun.

Es una *gran* nación.

It's a great country.

El presidente es un *gran* hombre.

The president is a great man.

A. Look at the sketches below. Write a phrase to describe each sketch. Use *gran* or *grandes* before the noun, *grande* or *grandes* after the noun.

MODELO: un libro

un libro grande   un gran libro

1. una escuela

_____ _____

2. un hombre

_____ _____

3. unos presidentes

_____ _____

4. unas amigas

_____ _____

5. un país

_____ _____

B. Write the correct form of *grande* in each blank, then translate each sentence.

MODELO: Es una ___*gran*___ clase. ___*It's a great class*___ .

1. George Washington era un _____ presidente.

_____

2. Los _____ libros están en la biblioteca.

_____

3. Los Ángeles es una ciudad _____ .

_____

4. Las muchachas no son _____ .

_____

5. Los Estados Unidos es un _____ país.

_____

Lección XIII — EL PROGRESIVO

GRAMÁTICA: Present participles and the present progressive tense

I. In English, verb forms that end in *-ing* are called present participles. In Spanish, present participles end in *-ando* or *-iendo*. To form them, drop the *-ar*, *-er*, or *-ir* from the infinitive and add *-ando* to *-ar* verbs and *-iendo* to *-er* or *-ir* verbs.

estudi*ar* - estudi*ando*   com*er* - com*iendo*   viv*ir* - viv*iendo*

A. Change the following infinitives to the present participle.

MODELO: estudiar *estudiando*

1. entrar _____
2. beber _____
3. aprender _____
4. ayudar _____
5. mirar _____

6. escribir _____
7. cantar _____
8. bailar _____
9. abrir _____
10. salir _____

B. Hidden in the maze are thirty Spanish verbs in the present participle form. Circle each and list them on the next page.

```
a  c  a  e  n  i  o  d  n  e  i  t  s  i  s  a
o  c  e  rr a  n  d  o  d  n  e  i  v  o  ll o
d  b  d  f  o  v  i  a  j  a  n  d  o  ll o  d
a  n  c  t  a  i  n  ñ  d  u  d  s  t  m  d  n
n  d  n  g  n  t  d  e  h  n  g  t  n  u  n  a
d  e  o  d  n  a  v  e  ll a  c  a  o  n  e  t
o  d  n  a  t  n  c  a  o  a  b  v  n  d  i  s
d  c  m  l  h  d  b  i  t  c  o  l  w  d  s  e
n  o  n  i  i  o  e  b  o  o  d  n  a  c  o  t
e  rr m  a  j  o  d  n  e  i  b  e  b  n  a  b
i  i  i  s  d  e  s  c  r  i  b  i  e  n  d  o
r  e  r  rr c  a  s  o  o  d  n  a  g  e  ll o
b  n  a  o  ll b  n  t  n  e  v  a  n  d  o  c
a  d  n  d  e  y  a  d  u  s  v  f  e  k  d  ll
v  o  d  n  a  s  u  n  o  d  n  a  c  s  u  b
i  t  o  e  a  w  o  d  n  e  i  v  i  v  h  j
e  g  u  i  n  o  d  n  a  t  l  a  s  g  t  i
n  n  d  m  i  n  i  o  d  n  e  i  n  o  p  e
d  t  e  o  o  t  r  a  b  a  j  a  n  d  o  m
o  n  n  c  d  n  v  g  r  i  t  a  n  d  o  v
```

1._____ 2._____ 3._____ 4._____
5._____ 6._____ 7._____ 8._____
9._____ 10._____ 11._____ 12._____
13._____ 14._____ 15._____ 16._____
17._____ 18._____ 19._____ 20._____
21._____ 22._____ 23._____ 24._____
25._____ 26._____ 27._____ 28._____
29._____ 30._____

C. Very few verbs are irregular in the present participle form. Among them are the following verbs:

Verbs with the stem ending in a vowel (except *i*): add *yendo*.

leer	le*yendo*
tr*a*er	tra*yendo*
c*a*er	ca*yendo*
infl*u*ir	influ*yendo*
o*í*r	o*yendo*
constr*u*ir	constru*yendo*
distrib*u*ir	distribu*yendo*

Other irregular present participles are:

ir	yendo
venir	viniendo
decir	diciendo
poder	pudiendo
seguir	siguiendo
servir	sirviendo
dormir	durmiendo

D. Complete the *crucigrama* with the present participle of the infinitive given.

HORIZONTALES	VERTICALES
5. distribuir	1. venir
7. decir	2. ir
9. traer	3. construir
10. oír	4. seguir
	6. poder
	8. caer

II. As you know, the simple present tense may express three ideas:

Habla - He talks, he is talking, he does talk

However, if you wish to emphasize the idea that the action is going on *right now,* the present progressive tense is used. The present progressive tense emphasizes the idea that the action is in progress, not that it happens as a general rule. To form the present progressive tense, combine the proper present tense form of *estar* with the present participle of the verb. It is a two-part verb.

Estoy hablando.   I'm talking.
Estás tocando el piano.   You're playing the piano.
Está lloviendo.   It's raining.
Estamos comiendo.   We're eating.
Están andando.   They're walking.

A. Complete the following sentences. Change the form of *estar* to agree with each new subject.

MODELO: Yo no estoy leyendo pero María _____

_____ *está leyendo.* _____

1. Paco no está cantando pero yo _____
2. Los niños no están nadando en la piscina pero las niñas _____
3. Alfredo no está jugando al fútbol pero Lupe _____
4. Uds. no están comiendo pero Marta y yo _____
5. No estoy escribiendo pero tú _____

B. Copy each of the following sentences next to the picture it matches on the next page.

Está lloviendo.   Está nevando.   Están bailando.
Está tocando la guitarra.   Está escribiendo.   Está comiendo.

MODELO: *Está tocando la guitarra* _____.

51

1. _____

2. _____

3. _____

4. _____

5. _____

C. Now be creative! Write an original Spanish sentence describing what is happening in each sketch. The following verbs will help you: *cantar, beber, jugar, correr, comer.*

MODELO: *María está tocando el violín.*

1. _____

2. _____

3. _____

4. _____

5. _____

D. Rewrite the following sentences. Change each verb from the present to the present progressive tense.

MODELO: Juan come mucho. _Juan está comiendo mucho_.

1. El profesor entra en la clase. _____
2. Tú no trabajas mucho. _____
3. Nadamos en el lago. _____
4. Toco el piano. _____
5. Los alumnos juegan al volibol. _____
6. Mi amigo escribe su lección. _____
7. Aprendemos el español. _____
8. Bebo una limonada. _____
9. No vives en un hotel. _____
10. Ellos no hacen nada. _____
11. ¿Qué dices? _____
12. Paco trae el libro. _____
13. Los hombres construyen una casa. _____
14. La nieve cae rápidamente. _____
15. ¿Qué oye Ud.? _____

III. When object pronouns are used with a present participle, they may be attached to the verb, or precede it.

Estoy lavando la ropa.   Estoy lavándo*la*.   *La* estoy lavando.

Rewrite the following sentences in the present progressive tense. Attach the object pronouns to the participle. Note the accent marks.

MODELO: Juan la escribe. _Juan está escribiéndola_.

1. Yo lo aprendo. _____
2. Tú la necesitas. _____
3. Paco las come. _____
4. Los ayudamos. _____
5. Los chicos la preparan. _____
6. Los chicos la oyen. _____
7. Mi mamá la dice. _____
8. Mis amigos los traen. _____
9. Lo sigues. _____
10. Los hombres las construyen. _____

Lección XIV — MÁS PROGRESIVOS

Gramática: The past progressive tense

I.   In lesson XIII you learned that the present progressive tense is used to describe an action that is going on right now. The same idea can be applied to the past. Instead of using the simple imperfect, we use the past progressive tense to emphasize that the action *was in progress* at a particular moment in the past. To form the past progressive tense, combine the imperfect tense form of *estar* with the present participle of the verb.

> Yo *estaba estudiando.*   I was studying.
> *Estabas hablando* por teléfono.   You were talking on the phone.
> Paco *estaba comiendo.*   Paco was eating.
> *Estábamos escuchando* la radio.   We were listening to the radio.
> Uds. *estaban corriendo.*   You were running.

A.   Write in the blanks the proper past progressive form of the verb in the model sentence.

Modelo: Paco estaba comiendo tacos.

Ud. y yo ___*estábamos comiendo*___ tacos.

1.   Paco estaba comiendo tacos.

Yo _____ tacos.

Mis amigos _____ tacos.

Ud. _____ tacos.

Tú y yo _____ tacos.

Tú _____ tacos.

2.   Anita estaba nadando en la piscina.

Uds. _____ en la piscina.

Yo _____ en la piscina.

Tú _____ en la piscina.

Mi amigo _____ en la piscina.

Nosotros _____ en la piscina.

B.   Rewrite the following sentences. Change the verb from the present progressive to the past progressive tense.

Modelo: Estoy hablando español. ___*Estaba hablando español*___ .

1.   ¿Estás cantando? _____

2.   Estamos visitando a Anita. _____

3.   Paco está comiendo. _____

4.   Estoy mirando la televisión. _____

5.   ¿Están Uds. comiendo? _____

C. Be creative! Write ten original Spanish sentences in the past progressive tense. Combine any subject you wish with the proper imperfect form of *estar* and any present participle. Choose a present participle phrase from the list or use any other verb you wish.

corriendo por el parque   escribiendo una carta
hablando español   tocando la guitarra
              jugando al baloncesto

MODELO: *Alberto estaba jugando al baloncesto* .

1. _____
2. _____
3. _____
4. _____
5. _____
6. _____
7. _____
8. _____
9. _____
10. _____

D. Answer the following questions. Use the present participle form of the verb illustrated.

MODELO: ¿Qué estabas haciendo? *Estaba jugando al golf* .

1. ¿Qué estabas haciendo?

   _____

   _____

2. ¿Qué estaba haciendo Juan?

   _____

   _____

3. ¿Qué estaban haciendo Uds.?

   _____

   _____

4. ¿Qué estaban haciendo las chicas?

   _____

   _____

5. ¿Qué estaba haciendo Carmen?

   _____

   _____

55

Lección XV — EL PERFECTO

GRAMÁTICA: Past participles and the present perfect tense

I.   In English, verb forms like done, gone, written, spoken, and seen are called past participles. A past participle always goes with an auxiliary or helping verb such as has or have.

In Spanish, past participles end in -ado or -ido. Drop the -ar, -er, or -ir from the infinitive and add -ado to -ar verbs and -ido to -er or -ir verbs.

hablar - hablado   comer - comido   vivir - vivido

A.   Change the following infinitives to their past participle form.

MODELO: Jugar ___jugado___

    1.   entrar _____   6.   vivir _____
    2.   beber _____   7.   cantar _____
    3.   aprender _____   8.   bailar _____
    4.   ayudar _____   9.   salir _____
    5.   mirar _____   10.   comer _____

B.   There are a few irregular past participles. Some of the most common are:

abrir - abierto (opened)   morir - muerto (died)
volver - vuelto (returned)   poner - puesto (put)
cubrir - cubierto (covered)   decir - dicho (said)
hacer - hecho (done, made)   ver - visto (seen)
escribir - escrito (written)   romper - roto (broken)

Complete the following *crucigrama* with the past participle forms of the verbs given.

HORIZONTALES

    5.   recibir
    7.   poner
    11.   abrir
    13.   usar
    18.   cantar
    19.   decir
    20.   comer
    21.   estar

VERTICALES

    1.   vivir
    2.   tocar
    3.   volver
    4.   escribir
    5.   romper
    6.   invitar
    8.   cubrir
    9.   morir
    10.   visitar
    12.   tocar
    14.   hacer
    15.   dar
    16.   ver
    17.   ser

C. The past participle is often used as an adjective. When used in this way, it agrees with the noun to which it refers.

> Miguel está *dormido*.　　Michael is asleep.
> Las cartas están *escritas*.　　The letters are written.
> La puerta está *abierta*.　　The door is open.
> Los libros están *cerrados*.　　The books are closed.

Rewrite the following sentences. Change the past participle to the past participle of the verb in parentheses. Be certain the past participle agrees with the noun in number and gender.

MODELO:　Mi hermana está dormida. (sentar)

Mi hermana está sentada　　　　　.

1.　El perro está muerto. (dormir)

_____

2.　La puerta está cerrada. (abrir)

_____

3.　La mesa no está puesta. (romper)

_____

4.　Las lecciones están escritas. (terminar)

_____

5.　Mis padres están sentados. (ocupar)

_____

57

II. The verb *haber* means to have (done something). It is an auxiliary or helping verb and can never stand alone. The present tense of *haber* is:

Yo - he   I have
Tú - has   You have
Él, Ella, Ud. - ha   He, she has, you have

Nosotros - hemos   We have

Ellos, Ellas, Uds. - han   They, you have

When the present tense of *haber* is combined with the past participle of another verb, the present perfect tense is formed. This tense tells what *has* happened. Notice that the past participle never changes its form when it follows *haber*.

He estudiado mucho.   I have studied a lot.
Mi gato *ha muerto*.   My cat has died.
No *hemos dicho* nada.   We haven't said anything.

A. Rewrite the following sentences. Change the form of *haber* to agree with each new subject.

MODELO: He nadado en el océano.

(Tú) _Has nadado en el océano_.

1. José ha nadado en el océano.

    (Tú) _____
    (Paco) _____
    (Uds.) _____
    (Mis amigos y yo) _____
    (Yo) _____

2. Paco ha comido demasiado.

    (Yo) _____
    (Uds.) _____
    (Mi amigo y yo) _____
    (Tú) _____
    (Papá) _____

B. Be creative! Write Spanish sentences describing what has happened in each sketch. Combine items from lists A, B, and C and write the complete sentence next to the sketch it describes.

MODELO: _Marta ha tocado la guitarra_.

A.	B.	C.	
Marta	ha	roto la piñata	dormido
Alfredo	han	tocado la guitarra	comido mucho
Los chicos		jugado al tenis	escrito cartas

58

1. _____
   _____

2. _____
   _____

3. _____
   _____

4. _____
   _____

5. _____
   _____

C. Read the questions below. Then write the missing words in the answers.

MODELO: ¿Quién ha llegado tarde? Conchita _ha_ _llegado_ tarde.

1. ¿Quién ha bailado contigo? Paco _____ _____ conmigo.

2. ¿Quiénes han ido contigo? Ellas _____ _____ conmigo.

3. ¿Quién ha terminado la lección? Yo _____ _____ la lección.

4. ¿Quiénes han entendido? Juan y yo _____ _____ .

5. ¿Ha salido el tren? Sí, el tren _____ _____ .

D. Answer the following questions with responses true for you.

MODELO: ¿A cuántas escuelas has asistido?

He asistido a tres escuelas .

1. ¿A cuántas escuelas has asistido?

   _____

2. ¿Han viajado tus padres a Europa?

   _____

3. En su opinión, ¿quién ha sido nuestro mejor presidente?

   _____

4. En su opinión, ¿cuál ha sido el mejor programa de televisión?

   _____

5. ¿En cuántas casas has vivido?

   _____

Lección XVI — MÁS PERFECTOS

GRAMÁTICA: The past perfect tense

I.   In lesson XV you have learned to use the present perfect tense to describe what has happened. The past perfect tense (sometimes called the pluperfect) tells what *had* happened prior to another event.

To form the past perfect tense, combine the imperfect form of *haber* with the past participle.

Yo *había viajado* a México.   I had traveled to Mexico.
Tú *habías viajado* a México.   You had traveled to Mexico.
Él *había viajado* a México.   He had traveled to Mexico.
Nosotros *habíamos viajado* a México.   We had traveled to Mexico.
Ellos *habían viajado* a México.   They had traveled to Mexico.

A.   Fill in the blanks with the proper form of *haber* in the imperfect.

MODELO: Yo __había__ llegado tarde.

1.   Paco _____ viajado a Europa.

2.   Tú y yo _____ terminado la conversación.

3.   Uds. _____ llegado temprano.

4.   Juan y Pepe _____ jugado al tenis.

5.   Yo _____ hablado con el profesor.

6.   Nosotros _____ ido a la fiesta.

7.   Tú _____ participado en el concierto.

8.   El profesor _____ llegado tarde a clase.

9.   Ud. _____ estado en mi casa.

10.   Los perros _____ muerto.

B.   Rewrite the following sentences. Change the verb from the present perfect to the past perfect tense.

MODELO: No he viajado a Europa. _No había viajado a Europa_ .

1.   ¿Has mirado la televisión? _____

2.   Mamá ha roto su lámpara favorita. _____

3.   Hemos estudiado para el examen. _____

4.   Los alumnos han sufrido un examen difícil. _____

5.   Siempre he dicho la verdad. _____

C.   Complete each sentence as in the model. Change each verb to the past perfect tense.

MODELO: Paco viajó a México el año pasado.

Antes _no había viajado_ .

1. Estudié para este examen. Antes _____

2. Juan bailó mucho anoche. Antes _____

3. Nadamos mucho el verano pasado. Antes _____

4. Tocaste el piano en la fiesta. Antes _____

5. Los niños me escribieron una carta la semana pasada.
   Antes _____

D. Be creative! Write ten original Spanish sentences in the past perfect tense. Combine any subject you wish with the proper imperfect form of *haber* and a past participle. Choose a past participle phrase from the list or use any other verb you wish: *llegado temprano, estudiado para el examen, recibido muchos regalos, escrito unas cartas, roto una piñata.*

MODELO: Mi amigo había roto una piñata _____ .

1. _____
2. _____
3. _____
4. _____
5. _____
6. _____
7. _____
8. _____
9. _____
10. _____

E. Answer the following questions. Use the correct verb and add the words suggested by the sketch.

MODELO: ¿Qué había comido el niño?

Había comido helado. _____

1. ¿A qué habías jugado?

   _____

2. ¿Qué habían estudiado los alumnos?

   _____

3. ¿Qué había roto el niño?

   _____

4. ¿Qué habían tocado Uds.?

   _____

5. ¿En qué estado habías vivido?

   _____

   TEXAS

61

Lección XVII — LOS MANDATOS

GRAMÁTICA: Affirmative and negative formal commands; familiar commands; irregular command forms; placement of object pronouns with commands

I. To form the polite (formal) command forms of regular Spanish verbs, simply reverse the final vowel of the present tense verb: *a* becomes *e*, and *e* becomes *a*. In other words, *-ar* verb commands will end in *-e* or *-en*, *-er* and *-ir* verb commands will end in *-a* or *-an*.

Ud. habl*a*.	You speak.	Habl*e* Ud.	Speak!
Uds. cant*an*.	You sing.	Cant*en* Uds.	Sing!
Ud. le*e*.	You read.	Le*a* Ud.	Read!
Uds. escrib*en*.	You write.	Escrib*an* Uds.	Write!

A. Rewrite the following sentences. Change from the statement to the command form.

MODELO: Ud. baila. _*Baile Ud.*_

1. Ud. bebe _____
2. Ud. come _____
3. Ud. lee _____
4. Uds. estudian _____
5. Ud. nada _____
6. Ud. abre _____
7. Uds. deciden _____
8. Uds. viven _____
9. Ud. permite _____
10. Uds. escuchan _____

11. Uds. bailan _____
12. Uds. contestan _____
13. Ud. entra _____
14. Ud. mira _____
15. Uds. venden _____
16. Uds. preguntan _____
17. Ud. escribe _____
18. Uds. trabajan _____
19. Uds. compran _____
20. Ud. ayuda _____

B. Most vowel-changing or irregular verbs form the command by dropping the *-o* of the *yo* form of the present tense. To this stem add *-e* or *-en* to *-ar* verbs and add *-a* or *-an* to *-er* or *-ir* verbs.

Infinitive	Yo form	Singular command	Plural command
cerr*ar*	cierr*o*	cierr*e* Ud.	cierr*en* Uds.
ten*er*	teng*o*	teng*a* Ud.	teng*an* Uds.

Write the present tense *yo* form of the infinitive given. Then write the singular and plural command forms.

MODELO: dormir yo _*duermo*_ _*duerma*_ Ud. _*duerman*_ Uds.

1. poner yo _____ _____ Ud. _____ Uds.
2. contar yo _____ _____ Ud. _____ Uds.
3. cerrar yo _____ _____ Ud. _____ Uds.
4. volver yo _____ _____ Ud. _____ Uds.
5. decir yo _____ _____ Ud. _____ Uds.

62

6. venir yo _____ _____ Ud. _____ Uds.

7. hacer yo _____ _____ Ud. _____ Uds.

8. ver yo _____ _____ Ud. _____ Uds.

9. salir yo _____ _____ Ud. _____ Uds.

10. pensar yo _____ _____ Ud. _____ Uds.

C. The following four verbs do not follow the rules previously given for command forms.

dar - dé Ud., den Uds.   ir - vaya Ud., vayan Uds.

saber - sepa Ud., sepan Uds.   ser - sea Ud., sean Uds.

Answer the following questions with the proper singular command response.

MODELO: ¿Me permite bailar? _Sí, ¡baile ud.!_____

1. ¿Me permite comer? _____

2. ¿Me permite volver? _____

3. ¿Me permite leer? _____

4. ¿Me permite empezar? _____

5. ¿Me permite entrar? _____

6. ¿Me permite ir? _____

7. ¿Me permite mirar? _____

8. ¿Me permite salir? _____

9. ¿Me permite escribir? _____

10. ¿Me permite escuchar? _____

D. Answer the following questions with the proper plural command forms.

MODELO: ¿Podemos bailar? _Sí, ¡bailen Uds.!_____

1. ¿Podemos ir? _____

2. ¿Podemos contar? _____

3. ¿Podemos venir? _____

4. ¿Podemos ver? _____

5. ¿Podemos ayudar? _____

E. Put it all together! Find, circle, and write on the lines the singular polite command form of each verb listed.

MODELO: trabajar _trabaje_

```
a  v  r  e  a  d  n  e  v  b  e  b  a  o
(t  r  a  b  a  j  e) m  r  e  d  a  n  m
e  e  d  y  t  h  l  c  o  m  a  t  p  q
i  r  n  e  a  p  e  s  u  a  t  s  r  r
d  t  a  g  i  s  a  b  a  d  i  c  e  d
u  n  a  g  a  a  y  u  d  e  m  o  g  e
t  e  s  q  l  a  g  i  d  u  r  n  u  s
s  v  e  n  g  a  b  n  t  e  e  t  n  c
e  o  u  l  b  e  s  n  e  i  p  e  t  r
m  e  rr e  i  c  r  a  e  t  o  s  e  i
i  b  a  i  l  e  u  p  r  i  n  t  s  b
r  o  a  v  i  v  o  e  m  b  g  e  b  a
e  s  c  r  i  b  a  l  n  o  a  f  l  o
h  a  b  l  e  t  n  a  c  t  c  l  t  u
i  s  t  a  f  e  ch u  c  s  e  q  b  o
```

dar _____	ir _____	saber _____	ser _____
tener _____	pensar _____	salir _____	hacer _____
venir _____	decir _____	volver _____	cerrar _____
contar _____	poner _____	ayudar _____	escuchar _____
comprar _____	permitir _____	ver _____	vivir _____
escribir _____	decidir _____	preguntar _____	abrir _____
vender _____	nadar _____	mirar _____	estudiar _____
entrar _____	leer _____	contestar _____	comer _____
bailar _____	beber _____	hablar _____	cantar _____

II. To form negative formal commands, simply place a *no* before the command form.

Bailen Uds.   *No* bailen Uds.
Cierre Ud. la puerta.   *No* cierre Ud. la puerta.

Rewrite the following statements changing each to a negative command.

MODELO: Ud. no puede cantar. _No cante Ud._

1. Ud. no puede entrar. _____

2. Uds. no pueden venir. _____

3. Uds. no pueden ir. _____

4. Ud. no puede comer. _____

5. Ud. no puede mirar. _____

III. Object pronouns are always attached to the end of direct affirmative commands.

Ponga el libro allí.   Pónga*lo* allí.
Invíten a mí.   Invíten*me*.

An accent mark must be used to keep the correct stress in pronunciation.

A. Rewrite the following sentences. Change the underlined noun to a pronoun.

MODELO: Beba Ud. la limonada. *Bébala* _____ .

1. Bailen Uds. el tango. _____

2. Conteste Ud. la pregunta. _____

3. Lean Uds. los libros. _____

4. Estudie Ud. las lecciones. _____

5. Cierren Uds. la puerta. _____

B. If there are two object pronouns, simply add both to the verb. Remember that the indirect precedes the direct object pronoun.

Cómpreme el libro.   Cómpre*melo*.

In the following sentences, replace both objects with the proper pronouns. Don't forget the accent mark.

MODELO: Compre el libro para Juan. *Cómpreselo* _____ .

1. Cómpreme la blusa. _____

2. Díganos la verdad. _____

3. Repítanme el cuento. _____

4. Hágale el favor para mamá. _____

5. Dele el regalo a Paco. _____

C. In a negative command, object pronouns go in their normal position before the verb.

No cierre Ud. la puerta. No *la* cierre Ud.

Rewrite the following commands. Change each from an affirmative to a negative command.

MODELO: Léalo Ud. *No lo lea Ud.* _____

1. Póngalos aquí. _____

2. Dígame. _____

3. Cómprelas. _____

4. Hágalo. _____

5. Repítanla. _____

IV. The affirmative command for *tú* is almost always the same as the *él, ella, Ud.* form of the present tense.

Mira - Look!   *Estudia* - Study!   *Repite* - Repeat!   *Piensa* - Think!

The eight irregular forms are:

venir - ven   tener - ten   poner - pon   salir - sal
hacer - haz   ser - sé   decir - di   ir - ve

Object pronouns are attached as with formal commands.

A. Write the *tú* command form of each of the following verbs.

MODELO: hablar __*habla*__

1. decir _____
2. venir _____
3. contar _____
4. escribir _____
5. ser _____

6. salir _____
7. beber _____
8. dar _____
9. tener _____
10. hacer _____

11. abrir _____
12. poner _____
13. leer _____
14. ir _____
15. contestar _____

B. Answer the following questions with the proper *tú* command form. Change each noun to the proper object pronoun.

MODELO: ¿Puedo beber la limonada? __Sí, ¡bébela!__

1. ¿Puedo comer los tacos? _____
2. ¿Puedo escribir la carta? _____
3. ¿Puedo comprar una bicicleta? _____
4. ¿Puedo decir la verdad? _____
5. ¿Puedo abrir las ventanas? _____

V. To form familiar negative commands, add an *s* to the polite commands.

Polite (Ud. form) command

No habl*e* Ud.
No lo beb*a*.

Familiar (tú form) command

No habl*es*.
No lo beb*as*.

A. Rewrite the following commands. Change from the *Ud.* form to the *tú* form.

MODELO: No la lea Ud. __No la leas__ .

1. No conteste Ud. _____
2. No entre Ud. _____
3. No venga Ud. _____
4. No escuche Ud. _____
5. No la cierre. _____

B. Rewrite the following commands. Change from the affirmative to the negative familiar command.

MODELO: ¡Estúdialo! _No lo estudies._

1. ¡Pregúntalo! _____
2. ¡Ven! _____
3. ¡Ponlos aquí! _____
4. ¡Ábrela! _____
5. ¡Dime! _____
6. ¡Escríbelos! _____
7. ¡Vete! _____
8. ¡Lee! _____
9. ¡Habla! _____
10. ¡Invítanos! _____

VI. Let's put it all together! Write four command forms of each verb given.

Infinitive	Formal commands		Familiar commands	
MODELO: hablar	_hable Ud._	_No hable Ud._	_Habla_	_No hables_
1. bailar				
2. comer				
3. salir				
4. ir				
5. escribir				
6. abrir				
7. poner				
8. cerrar				
9. hacer				
10. cantar				

Lección XVIII — EL FUTURO

GRAMÁTICA: The future tense of regular and irregular verbs

I.   The future tense tells what will or shall happen. The endings are added on to the whole infinitive. The same set of endings is used for all verbs. Note the accent marks.

Person	Ending	Example: hablar, comer, vivir
Yo	é	hablaré, comeré, viviré
Tú	ás	hablarás, comerás, vivirás
Él, Ella, Ud.	á	hablará, comerá, vivirá
Nosotros	emos	hablaremos, comeremos, viviremos
Ellos, Ellas, Uds.	án	hablarán, comerán, vivirán

A.   Write in the blanks the proper future tense form of the verb given at the top of each list.

MODELO: *estudiar*   Yo ___estudiaré___

1.   *jugar* - to play
Yo _____
Uds. _____
Anita _____
Tú y yo _____
Tú _____

2.   *trabajar* - to work
Tú _____
Los alumnos _____
Ud. _____
Yo _____
Nosotros _____

3.   *dormir* - to sleep
Nosotras _____
Tú _____
Yo _____
Mis padres _____
Paco _____

4.   *beber* - to drink
Juan y yo _____
Los alumnos _____
Ud. _____
Tú _____
Yo _____

B.   Complete the following sentences with the correct future tense form of the verb in parentheses.

MODELO: (hablar) Alicia ___hablará___ español.

1.   (dar) Los amigos _____ una fiesta para Ana.

2.   (abrir) Yo _____ esta puerta.

3.   (ir) ¿_____ Uds. a la fiesta?

4.   (nadar) Nosotros _____ mañana.

5.   (ser) ¿Qué día _____ ?

6.   (comer) Mis amigos y yo _____ demasiado.

7.   (jugar) Yo _____ al tenis.

8.   (cerrar) ¿ _____ tú las ventanas?

9.   (beber) Tú _____ café con leche.

10.   (preguntar) El profesor _____ mucho.

II. Few Spanish verbs are irregular in the future tense. The endings are the same, but they are added to a shortened form of the infinitive.

Verb	Shortened form	Future forms
venir	vendr-	vendré, vendrás . . .
tener	tendr-	tendré, tendrás . . .
poner	pondr-	pondré, pondrás . . .
salir	saldr-	saldré, saldrás . . .
poder	podr-	podré, podrás . . .
saber	sabr-	sabré, sabrás . . .
hacer	har-	haré, harás . . .
decir	dir-	diré, dirás . . .
querer	querr-	querré, querrás . . .

A. Rewrite the following sentences. Change each verb form to agree with the new subject.

MODELO: Paco vendrá mañana. Yo _vendré mañana._

1. Los alumnos tendrán prisa.

   Tú _____

2. Pondremos los libros allí.

   Yo _____

3. Saldrás mañana.

   Paco _____

4. No podré ir.

   Nosotros _____

5. Mamá sabrá la verdad.

   Mis padres _____

6. ¿Qué harán Uds.?

   ¿ _____ tú?

7. Yo diré la verdad.

   Nosotros _____

8. ¿Querrás ir?

   ¿ _____ Uds.?

9. ¿A qué hora vendrán Uds.?

   ¿ _____ tú?

10. Paco no hará nada.

    Mis amigos _____

B. *Crucigrama:* Complete the puzzle with the proper future tense form of the verb given.

HORIZONTALES

2. decir - nosotros
5. hacer - él
8. venir - nosotros
14. poner - ellos
15. querer - ella
16. decir - Ud.
17. poder - nosotros

VERTICALES

1. querer - nosotros
2. decir - ellos
3. saber - Ud.
4. saber - nosotros
6. poder - ellos
7. tener - ellos
9. salir - ellos
10. salir - yo
11. venir - tú
12. hacer - ellos
13. poner - yo

III. Rewrite each sentence. Change the verb from the present to the future tense.

Modelo: Hablo español. _Hablaré español_ .

1. Los alumnos leen mucho. _____
2. Venimos a las diez. _____
3. Los niños salen a las 11.00. _____

4. Comes el almuerzo temprano. _____

5. Estamos en casa. _____

6. No puedo ir. _____

7. Es lunes. _____

8. Paco no sabe la verdad. _____

9. Juegas al tenis. _____

10. Vamos a la clase. _____

IV. Answer the following questions. Use the proper future tense form of the verb suggested by the sketch.

jugar al béisbol   **tocar el piano**   **salir a las once**

comer los tacos   **leer los libros**

MODELO: ¿Qué harán Uds. mañana? *Leeremos los libros* .

1.   ¿Qué harás mañana?

_____

2.   ¿Qué harán Uds. mañana?

_____

3.   ¿Qué harán los niños?

_____

4.   ¿Qué harás mañana?

_____

5.   ¿Qué hará Paco mañana?

_____

Lección XIX — EL POTENCIAL

GRAMÁTICA: Conditional tense of *-ar*, *-er*, *-ir* verbs

I.   The conditional tense tells what would or should happen (if . . .). Just like the future tense, the conditional is formed by adding *one* set of endings to the whole infinitive. The endings are the same as those for the imperfect tense of *-er* or *-ir* verbs.

Person	Ending		Person	Ending
Yo	- ía		Nosotros	- íamos
Tú	- ías			
Él, Ella, Ud.	- ía		Ellos, Ellas, Uds.	- ían

For example:

comprar	Yo compr*aría*.	I would buy.
comer	Tú com*erías*.	You would eat.
vivir	Paco viv*iría*.	Paco would live.

The verbs that are irregular in the future are also irregular in the conditional. The infinitive and *yo* form in the conditional are listed below.

venir - vendría	tener - tendría	poner - pondría
salir - saldría	poder - podría	saber - sabría
hacer - haría	decir - diría	querer - querría

A.   Write the proper conditional tense forms of the following verbs.

MODELO: (hablar) Yo _hablaría_ .

1.   (saber) Tú _____

2.   (trabajar) Yo _____

3.   (permitir) Mi amigo y yo _____

4.   (hacer) Paco _____

5.   (ir) Uds. _____

6.   (poder) Mis amigos _____

7.   (tocar) Yo _____

8.   (venir) Ud. _____

9.   (visitar) Nosotros _____

10.   (escribir) Tú _____

B.   Complete each sentence with the proper verb in the conditional tense.

MODELO: Paco no estudió aunque dijo que _estudiaría_.

1.   Yo no terminé el libro aunque dije que _____

2.   No tocaste el piano aunque dijiste que _____

72

3. Mi amigo no vino aunque dijo que _____

4. No fuimos a la fiesta aunque dijimos que _____

5. No jugaron al tenis aunque dijeron que _____

C. Rewrite the following sentences. Change the underlined verb to the one given in parentheses.

MODELO: ¿Qué harían Uds.?

(decir) _¿Qué dirían Uds.?_

1. Me prometió que la buscaría.

   (explicar) _____

2. Yo dije que contestaría la carta.

   (leer) _____

3. Dijimos que escribiríamos la lección.

   (aprender) _____

4. Me prometiste que limpiarías la ropa.

   (lavar) _____

5. Mis padres dijeron que iríamos a México.

   (viajar) _____

D. Be creative! Write a short paragraph describing what you would do if you had all the money you would need. Write at least five sentences using the conditional tense. The following verbs may help you: *comprar, viajar, visitar, vivir, ir, dar, ayudar, tener.*

_____

_____

_____

_____

_____

E. Now rewrite the paragraph you wrote in part D. Tell what we would do and change each verb to the *nosotros* form.

_____

_____

_____

_____

_____

F. Look at each sketch on the next page, then read the question next to it. Decide what you would do in each situation and write your answer on the line.

MODELO: ¿Irías a la playa o irías al cine?

Yo iría a la playa.

1. ¿Jugarías al béisbol o esquiarías?

_____

2. ¿Andarías a la escuela o tomarías un autobús?

_____

3. ¡EXAMEN MAÑANA! ¿Estudiarías o mirarías la televisión?

_____

4. ¿Limpiarías el dormitorio o visitarías a tus amigos?

_____

5. ¿Jugarías al tenis o montarías en bicicleta?

_____

G. Answer the following questions affirmatively if you think you would do what is asked. Answer negatively if not.

MODELO: ¿Llevarías un traje de baño a la escuela?

No llevaría un traje de baño a la escuela .

1. ¿Estudiarías para un examen importante?

_____

2. ¿Hablarías por teléfono por dos horas?

_____

3. ¿Dormirías en las clases?

_____

4. ¿Bailarías mucho en una fiesta?

_____

5. ¿Comprarías una motocicleta?

_____

Lección XX — PALABRAS INTERESANTES

GRAMÁTICA: Spanish word families, common suffixes, prefixes and cognates

I.   Many Spanish nouns are formed by dropping the *r* from the infinitive. Add *-dor* or *-dora* to form the noun.

juga*r* - to play   juga*dor* - player (m.)   juga*dora* - player (f.)

A.   Write the nouns formed from the following verbs.

MODELO: jugar   *jugador*   *jugadora*

1. descubrir   _____   _____
2. libertar   _____   _____
3. conquistar   _____   _____
4. pescar   _____   _____
5. observar   _____   _____
6. boxear   _____   _____

B.   Other nouns are formed by adding *-a* to the English word.

dentist   - el dentist*a*, la dentist*a*

The gender is indicated by the article *el* or *la*.
Write the Spanish nouns formed from the following words.

MODELO: artist   *el artista*   *la artista*

1. motorist   _____   _____
2. guitarist   _____   _____
3. realist   _____   _____
4. optimist   _____   _____
5. idealist   _____   _____

C.   Many of the nouns that end in *-tion* in English, end in *-ción* in Spanish. Most of these nouns are feminine.

na*tion* - la na*ción*

To make these nouns plural, add *-es* to the word: las nacion*es*.

Write the Spanish nouns formed from these English nouns.

MODELO: nation   *la nación*   *las naciones*

1. operation   _____   _____
2. cooperation   _____   _____
3. invitation   _____   _____
4. conversation   _____   _____
5. education   _____   _____

D. Some English nouns that end in *-ce* appear in Spanish with the ending *-cia*.

conferen*ce* - conferen*cia*

Write the Spanish words formed from these English nouns.

MODELO: independence *independencia*

1. justice _____
2. notice _____
3. distance _____
4. residence _____
5. importance _____

E. Other nouns end in *-cio*. Write these Spanish nouns.

MODELO: palace *palacio*

1. silence _____
2. sacrifice _____
3. service _____
4. novice _____
5. precipice _____

F. English adverbs ending in *-ly* often end in *-mente* in Spanish: *rapidly - rápidamente*. Write these adverbs in Spanish.

MODELO: generally *generalmente*

1. directly _____
2. totally _____
3. personally _____
4. especially _____
5. finally _____

II. Some Spanish prefixes and suffixes

To indicate smallness or cuteness, or as an endearing nickname, the suffix *-ito* or *-ita* is often added to many nouns or adjectives.

momento - moment*ito*   casa - cas*ita*

A. Add the suffix *-ito* or *-ita* to the following words.

MODELO: minuto *minutito*

1. libro _____
2. cama _____
3. plato _____
4. papel _____
5. toro _____

6. regalo _____
7. abuela _____
8. hermana _____
9. Juana _____
10. Juan _____

B. The suffix *-miento* will turn some Spanish verbs into nouns.

pensar - to think   pensa*miento* - thought

Write the nouns formed from the following verbs.

MODELO: casar _casamiento_

1. tratar _____
2. llamar _____
3. levantar _____
4. mandar _____
5. conocer _____

C. The suffix *-dad* will turn some adjectives into nouns.

enfermo - sick   enferme*dad* - sickness

Make nouns out of the following adjectives.

MODELO: seguro _seguridad_

1. relativo _____
2. sincero _____
3. oportuno _____
4. tranquilo _____
5. nervioso _____

D. The suffix *-al* will turn many nouns into adjectives.

nación - nacion*al*

Make adjectives out of these nouns.

MODELO: centro _central_

1. profesión _____
2. educación _____
3. flor _____
4. idea _____
5. medicina _____

E. The prefixes *des-* and *in-* reverse the meaning of the noun.

orden - order   acción - action   dependiente - dependent

*des*orden - disorder   *in*acción - inaction   *in*dependiente - independent

Add the prefix *des–* to these nouns.

1. unión _____   4. esperar _____
2. ventaja _____   5. organizar _____
3. conocer _____

Add the prefix *in–* to these nouns.

1. competencia _____
2. oportunidad _____
3. seguridad _____

4. decisión _____
5. directo _____

F. The name of a person who makes or sells a certain item can be derived by adding *-ero* or *-era* to the noun.

   zapato - shoe   zapat*ero* - shoemaker   zapat*era* - shoemaker

To get the name of a store selling the item, add *–ería* to the noun.

   zapato   zapat*ería* - shoe store

Complete the following word families.

MODELO: zapato ___*zapatero*_____   ___*zapatería*___

1. joya _____ _____
2. flor _____ _____
3. camisa _____ _____
4. fruta _____ _____
5. libro _____ _____
6. papel _____ _____
7. tortilla _____ _____
8. pan _____ _____
9. leche _____ _____
10. carne _____ _____